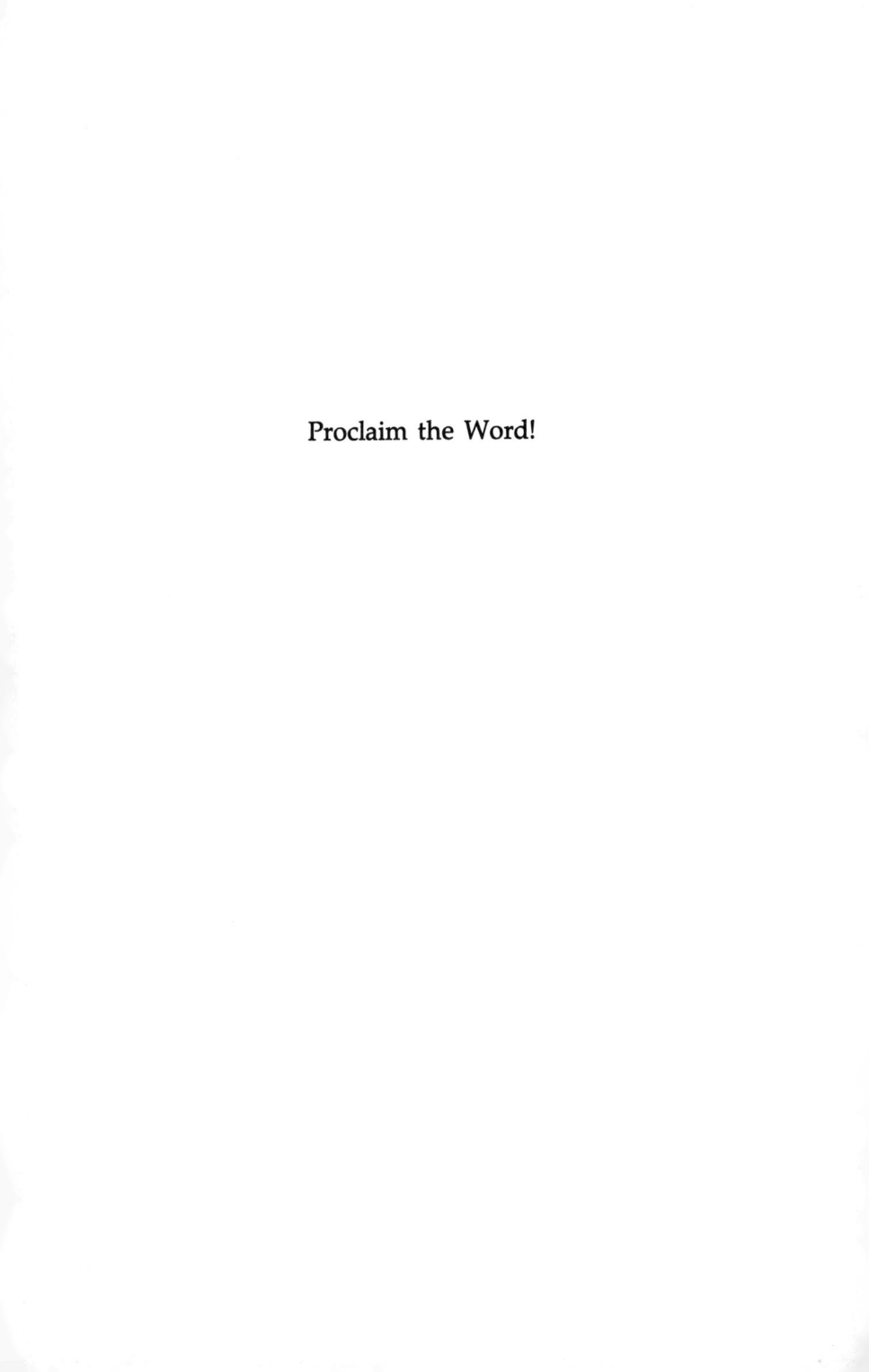

Proclaim the Word!

# Proclaim the WORD!

E. Eugene Hall
James L. Heflin

**BROADMAN PRESS**
Nashville, Tennessee

TO OUR WIVES
Reba Frances Hall
and
Wilma R. Heflin
loving companions in the service of God

© Copyright 1985 • Broadman Press
All rights reserved
4221-02
ISBN: 0-8054-2102-5
Dewey Decimal Classification: 251
Subject Heading: PREACHING
Library of Congress Catalog Card Number: 84-1745-8
Printed in the United States of America

Unless otherwise noted, Scripture quotations are from the Revised Standard Version of the Bible, copyrighted 1946, 1952, © 1971, 1973.

Scripture quotations marked (KJV) are from the King James Version of the Bible

**Library of Congress Cataloging in Publication Data**

Hall, E. Eugene, (Ernest Eugene)
   Proclaim the word!

   Bibliography: p.
   Includes index.
   1. Preaching.   I. Heflin, James L., 1943–
II. Title.
BV4211.2.H24   1985       251        84-17458
ISBN 0-8054-2102-5

# Foreword

The first disciples were commissioned and recommissioned for their task. Jesus gave the commission we characterize as *great:* "Go therefore and make disciples of all nations, baptizing them in the name of the Father and of the Son and of the Holy Spirit, teaching them to observe all that I have commanded you" (Matt. 28:19-20*a*). In his Gospel, Luke stated the commission within Jesus' final teaching about the answered prophecies of the Messiah's suffering, death, and resurrection, "repentance and forgiveness of sins should be preached in his name to all nations, beginning from Jerusalem. You are witnesses of these things" (24:46-48). Jesus restated the commission in Acts, "But you shall receive power when the Holy Spirit has come upon you; and you shall be my witnesses in Jerusalem and in all Judea and Samaria and to the end of the earth" (1:8).

The response to the commission came immediately following the empowering gift of the Holy Spirit: "But Peter standing with the eleven, lifted up his voice and addressed them" (Acts 2:14). Peter preached, responded to questions (v. 38), testified, and exhorted (v. 40). Further, the apostles were God's agents for healing and mediating encouragement to fellowship, frequently about the table. Also, the apostles were involved in the setting of priorities and offering of prayer and praise.

Ironically the blessing of their ministry led to resentment and jealousy among those who were the established religious leaders of that day. Arrest, imprisonment, and intimidation were the tools employed to discourage these preachers. Upon their imprisonment following their bold ministry within the environs of the Temple, the messenger of God brought both their release and a word of recommissioning altogether in keeping with the prior statements: "Go and stand in the temple and speak to the people all the words of this Life" (5:20). The verbs are instructive: *go, stand,* and *speak.*

Our task in addressing the commission of present day apostles (ones sent to represent their Lord) is to focus upon standing to speak "all the words of this Life," with boldness (4:31) and joy (5:41).

*Proclaim the Word! The Bases of Preaching* we offer to those who stand and speak with the prayer that through our response to the commission of our Lord, God may continue to add to our number day by day those who are being saved.

# Contents

1. The Theological Basis of Preaching..................1
2. The Personal Basis of Preaching......................25
3. The Social Basis of Preaching..........................42
4. The Logical Basis of Preaching........................77
5. The Inventive Basis of Preaching...................102
6. The Ideational Basis of Preaching..................126
7. The Structural Basis of Preaching..................148
8. The Expressive Basis of Preaching.................178
9. The Communicative Basis of Preaching...........213
    Indexes..................................................250

# 1
## The Theological Basis of Preaching

The preacher stands to proclaim the Word. Who is the *preacher?* What is *proclamation?* What do we mean by *the* Word? *Proclaim the Word!* begins with these questions because we are convinced that the preacher before he begins to preach must know what preaching is, what its subject matter is, and what it is designed to accomplish.

### A Biblical Definition of Preaching

What is preaching? is a theological question whose answer must precede attention to technique in the study of proclamation.[1] Preaching should have a broader theoretical base than that afforded by a definition of the term followed by a discussion of "how-to" prepare sermons. Preaching definitions abound and offer valid perspectives. The most notable of them (those of Brooks, Broadus, and Blackwood to cite three which are well known) grow out of one basic idea: *Preaching is the communication of God's Word to persons.* Moreover, *preaching is the task of a messenger who speaks the Word with a view to gaining a response.*

We must begin, then, with the understanding that

preaching is the speaking of God's Word in human words. Yet, there is something even more basic—we must first understand the nature of God's Word itself.

**Word as Deed**

The Word of God is a deed revealed at the very beginning of the Bible in the account of creation. The language depicts the Word of God as something done: it is not mere speech. The Word of God is speech combined with action. God said, "Let there be light," and there was light (Gen. 1:3). The creative power of the Word accomplished what God spoke.

The prophets described God's Word as a living, moving, compelling word. Repeatedly in the call of the prophet, we read: "The word of the Lord came to me" (Ezek. 6:1). Jeremiah dramatically describes the power released with the Word of God: It is "like a hammer which breaks the rock in pieces" (Jer. 23:29).

The New Testament also explains God's Word in terms of action: "The Word became flesh and dwelt among us" (John 1:14). Paul thanked God for the Thessalonians because they received the Word of God "not as the word of men, but as what it really is, the word of God, which is at *work* in you believers" (1 Thess. 2:13, authors' italics).

**Word as Message**

In addition, the Word of God is a message to be delivered. The Hebrews did not associate *dabar* (to speak) with events only; they also understood it as speech.[2] Prophets felt a compulsion to speak because they were instructed to do so and because of an inner

# The Theological Basis of Preaching

working of the Word of God, described as a consuming fire (Jer. 1:7; 20:9). The prophet, thus, had to speak.

Furthermore, the emphasis on the Word as speech in the New Testament is equally strong. Jesus declared that his own mission was "[to] preach" (Mark 1:38). Luke gives us the record of Jesus's first sermon, in which he announced: "The Spirit of the Lord is upon me,/because he has anointed me to preach" (see Luke 4:16-21 for the complete statement). Paul expressed a deep conviction about preaching. He assured the Thessalonians that God had given him the gospel *to speak* (1 Thess. 2:4).

At the highest point of revelation, God brought event and word together in his Son: "In many and various ways God spoke of old to our fathers by the prophets; but in these last days he has spoken to us by a Son" (Heb. 1:1-2).

Biblical theology gives these insights into the nature of the Word.[3] In preaching we speak again the word of God. Does that mean that the preacher in speaking has released the Word to do its work again? Is preaching more than speaking? An affirmative answer means that preaching is a message of redemption, but it is more.[4]

New Testament words translated "to preach" add significantly to the understanding of preaching. The most common words are: *proclaim*, or *herald; to tell good news* (with the emphasis on the content of the news); *to declare* and *to witness*.[5] Among these the word *proclaim* occurs most often. It means to herald forth a message. The herald, a personal representative of the monarch, is responsible for delivering the message.

In the centuries following New Testament times, preaching has been described as a special kind of public speaking. Volumes written to instruct preachers in the art of public speaking assert that preaching is nothing more or less than "sacred rhetoric." These authors compare the preparation of sermons to the preparation of speeches (more or less equating the two). Yet, the sermon has a peculiar quality about it which no other form of public address has. Something occurs in preaching that happens at no other time. That mysterious occurrence is the Divine work. An attempt to formulate the theological basis of preaching is an attempt to describe the working of God through the human words of the sermon.

These theological insights into the Word of God are essential to our understanding our task. The minister speaks for God to persons in order that he may bring them to Christ. Our employing theological terms, such as *God's creative and redemptive activity*, suggests that preaching while a practical discipline is also a theological discipline. Preparing and preaching a sermon is no small matter.

The preacher should remember that when he preaches a sermon he represents God to people. This thought fills us with awe. He who dares to preach sermons must find solid theological ground upon which to stand. With Paul we ask, "Who is sufficient for these things?" (2 Cor. 2:16). No human is really sufficient. Yet, God calls humans, you and me, to preach. He speaks His Word anew through our words when we come before the people to preach.

### Old Testament Preaching

A brief review of the nature of preaching in the Old Testament will increase our understanding of our

## The Theological Basis of Preaching

calling. The Hebrew word for *prophet* basically means "a spokesman for God." Because God called him, gave him a message, and instructed him to deliver it to the people, the prophet spoke. "Hear the Word of the Lord" was the theme of the prophet. What was the content of his message?

First, the message was a statement of God's intent. Jeremiah, for example, told King Zedekiah that Babylon would conquer Jerusalem. The sins of God's people were so great that God could not spare them from His wrath (Jer. 37:17). The content of the declaration was the will and intent of God.

The prophets strongly identified with God and His purpose. In numerous passages of Jeremiah and Ezekiel, the interpreter has difficulty determining whether God or the prophet is speaking. The symbolic actions of those two prophets in particular reveal the grief of God who had been betrayed by His people. The prophets sometimes actually embodied and personified the spirit of the messages they bore.

Second, the message was a warning about judgment. Though it was no easy word to speak, the prophets thundered against social and personal evil in Israel. Among the eighth-century prophets, Amos stands out. He inveighed against injustice and declared that God's wrath was a certainty if repentance did not occur quickly.

Jeremiah had the sad duty of pronouncing judgment on Judah (as Amos, Isaiah, Hosea, and Micah had done in Israel). One who reads Jeremiah discovers quickly that the prophet knew the heart of God. It was a burdensome duty, and Jeremiah really did not want to do it; but he was compelled to speak.

Third, the message was a promise for the future. Isaiah is probably the best known of the foretellers. In chapters 7, 9, and 11 of his prophecy, Isaiah spoke of the one who was to come. These beautiful and meaningful passages foretold the coming of the Messiah and the completion of God's purpose for His people. The failures of Israel would not thwart the plans of God. He employed the prophets (especially those of the eighth century) to reveal the truth to Israel that there is hope within the providence of God.

Each of the prophets was fearless, bold, confident, and certain of his message. The content rarely was misunderstood. Under divine command, the prophet played a major role in revealing God's purpose for Israel. The power of the spoken Word of God is evident in the ministries of the prophets.

There is, however, another aspect of the ministry of the Word in the Old Testament. Edmund Clowney points to the teaching of the revealed word as an often overlooked dimension of Old Testament preaching.[6] The primary responsibility for teaching belonged to the priests, although the prophets, the judges, the kings, and the fathers had similar responsibilities.

The dynamic quality of God's word is revealed in creation and in the history of redemption as declared by the prophets. The words of God as law were set down and placed in the ark of the covenant. The covenant, a formal, objective written instrument, is God's word present among his people (Ex. 30:11-14). According to Clowney, there never was any antithesis between the free spirit and the fixed letter with respect to God's word. The covenant, the *torah*, instructed Israel in the

## The Theological Basis of Preaching

ways of their God just as did the spoken word of the prophets.[7]

The primary example of the teaching aspect of the ministry of the Word in the Old Testament is found in Ezra the priest. When the Jews returned from Babylonian Exile to rebuild their city and Temple, Ezra read the words of the Law to them and enlisted the scribes to help him explain them to the people (Neh. 8). Reading and explaining the words of the Law later became the pattern of synagogue preaching (Luke 4:16-21). This "running commentary" on Scripture, talking through the meaning of the recorded Word, is the earliest and, the dominant preaching form until Christian preachers came under the influence of Greek rhetoric.

The twofold aspect of the ministry of the word in the Old Testament has direct implications for the contemporary pastor. He combines the two functions in one office: he must preach and teach.

### New Testament Preaching

Our understanding of preaching also can be increased by a review of the role of the prophet as apostle in the New Testament. The prophet who bridged the gap between the Testaments was John the Baptist. John was "sent from God . . . to bear witness to the light, that all might believe through him" (John 1:6-7). John preached a message of repentance and baptism based on that repentance and subsequent confession. Also, he had the singular honor of announcing to the world that Jesus had come to take away the sin of the world (John 1:29).

John understood his own ministry to be the fulfillment of a promise by the Old Testament prophet Isaiah (Mark

1:2-8; Isa. 40:3). He came to prepare the way for the Lord. From the time of John's ministry, the concept of the prophet as *one sent from God* again became dominant. Like the prophets before him, John had a deep conviction that God had called him, had given him a message, and had directed him to speak.

John's message included denunciation of sin and warnings about the wrath of God with the call for repentance. He also stressed the high standard of morality required by a righteous God. His bold message eventually cost him his life (Matt. 14:1-12).

The primary feature of John's preaching was the declaration that Christ would come and that, as the forerunner, John had only come to prepare the way. Refusing the temptation to declare himself Messiah, John pointed to Jesus as the ideal prophet, the Christ, the Lamb of God (John 1:19-42). He extolled the virtues of Christ and minimized his own role (John 3:30). One of the most poignant compliments Jesus paid to a person He gave to John the Baptist (Matt. 11:7-15).

Jesus also was *one sent from God*. He announced to His disciples, "As the Father hath sent me, even so I send you" (John 20:21). These words came near the close of our Lord's earthly ministry yet He was aware of that commission from the beginning. The first three Gospel writers stated early in their books that Jesus came preaching (Matt. 4:17; Mark 1:38; Luke 4:16-21). Mark recorded that Jesus declared to His disciples that He should not remain in one place but should go into other towns to "preach there also: for that is why I came out" (1:38). In Luke's Gospel, Jesus boldly revealed that He came to fulfill prophecy and to proclaim good news.

## The Theological Basis of Preaching

The word *preach* occurs three times in two verses (4:18-19).

Christ was the ideal prophet sent from God with authority and power. When Christ ascended to the Father, He committed His ministry to His followers and sent them into the world: The prophet and the apostle merge. They understood their mission to include preaching "repentance and forgiveness of sins . . . in his name to all nations, beginning from Jerusalem" (Luke 24:47).

Early in the Book of Acts, the preaching of Simon Peter is central. He responded to Christ's commission as a sent one or apostle with the task to preach. Perhaps Peter's most famous sermon was the one he preached on the day of Pentecost (Acts 2:14-40). After that miraculous day, Peter and John witnessed in Jerusalem continually. In the streets and in the Temple, Peter boldly called on the people to repent and be converted (Acts 3:19). Peter was reluctant to go beyond Jerusalem at first; but after receiving explicit instructions from God, he went to Caesarea to preach in the house of Cornelius (Acts 10:1-43). Gradually the gospel broke out of the confines of Jerusalem as Peter and others obeyed the voice of God.

Paul, identified often as "an apostle," is perhaps the best known of all New Testament preachers except for Christ. His dramatic conversion is a source of inspiration to Christians everywhere (Acts 9:1-19). For three days after his conversion, Paul was blind and did not eat or drink. Then Ananias went to Damascus, put his hands on Paul, and informed him that he would receive his sight and the Holy Ghost. Paul received his sight, was baptized, and ate. After "certain days" with the disciples at Damascus, immediately Paul began to preach (Acts 9:19-20). Later, he and Barnabas were set apart by the church at Antioch for the work God had called them to do. They "being sent out by the Holy Spirit," sailed to Cyprus and at Salamis "proclaimed the word of God in the synagogues of the Jews" (Acts 13:4-5).

Paul, like Jesus, John the Baptist, and Peter, was a man on mission. Ever conscious of his assignment, he proclaimed Christ in all the places where he went. He took Timothy into his evangelistic troupe and grew fond enough of the young preacher to think of him as a son in the ministry. Among the last words Paul wrote to Timothy were these: "Preach the word . . . . Do the work of an evangelist" (2 Tim. 4:2-5).

In the preaching of the apostles the sermon and the gospel were one. There was one message: "He lives." The essential nature of the *kerygma*, the gospel preached in the New Testament church, focused upon the death, resurrection, and exaltation of Jesus; the evaluation of Jesus as both Lord and Christ; and a call to repent and receive forgiveness of sins.

Who could possess firsthand knowledge of the central event in salvation history and refrain from going to tell the good news? The resurrection validated for his followers everything that Jesus said. Thus, the resurrection informs the character of preaching: It gives us our basis for understanding preaching as God's power at work. The resurrection tells us how God's revelation of his plan became complete. The *kerygma*, the gospel story, is the heart of Christian preaching.

The sermon emerged as the preacher's witness to the resurrection. It is "a unique form of discourse because the Word it proclaims is unique."[8] The sermon is the gospel with all its implications.

## Preaching in the History of the Church

The history of preaching parallels the history of the church whose ministers shaped the form and content of Christian proclamation. The fires ignited by the tongues of flame at Pentecost continued to burn brightly throughout the New Testament era. There was an urgency about the proclamation of the risen Lord. The few sermons we have recorded in the New Testament are simple but profound.

After the passing of the first apostles, preachers proclaimed the Christ they had heard about from eyewitnesses. This new emphasis in preaching did not deter the spread of Christianity throughout the Mediterranean world. Paul established churches while on his missionary journeys (Acts 13—20). He appointed elders in those churches to preach and to provide care for the believers.

Jewish Christians founded other congregations as they were dispersed following the destruction of Jerusalem in AD 70. Peter wrote to those congregations in Asia Minor (1 Pet. 1:1-2) and, like Paul, stressed the importance of feeding the flock (1 Pet. 5:1-4). The spread of the church and its continued existence give evidence that faithful preachers proclaimed the Word and strengthened the church through teaching.

Toward the end of the second century, the spread of Christianity occasioned changes in the content of preaching. Christian spokesmen dealt with a continuing evangelistic purpose but became concerned as well with matters of theology—doctrine and the canon of Scripture—and with church polity. The first church buildings were constructed and the first formal orders of worship were developed.

The mantle of leadership in proclamation during the next three hundred years of Christian history fell upon Justin Martyr, Clement of Alexandria, Tertullian, Origen, Cyprian, Gregory of Nazianzus, Basil the Great, Ambrose, Augustine and Chrysostom, among others.[9] Justin Martyr and other apologists defended the church and the faith against critics and persecutors. Throughout the Roman Empire, there were rival beliefs vying for the allegiance of the populace. The apologists spoke for the faith, defining it and giving positive witness to it.

Although Rome held the military power and its political system spread throughout the world, Greek was the language of culture and commerce. Hellenism dominated education and culture. One of the major emphases of Greek education, rhetoric, had a profound influence on preaching and sermon form by adding ordered and reasoned defense of the faith to the presentation of biblical content.

The preaching of Augustine, Bishop of Hippo, and John Chrysostom of Antioch led to the growth of two centers of influence upon preaching in the church. When the great schism occurred in the church, resulting in the formation of the Roman Catholic Church and the Eastern Orthodox Church, form and order in worship overshadowed proclamation in both branches of Christianity. The sacraments became the rival to preaching. In time, the sermon almost disappeared from the liturgy. The primary reason for this development, according to Dewitte T. Holland, was that clergy had little or no preparation for preaching and they began to do just what they were trained to do—preside over the liturgy.[10] As Christianity gained ascendancy in the West, the church became more of an institution than a vital force. Church leaders occupied their time with secular matters instead of preaching. The power of the pulpit diminished as the proclamation of the gospel declined in importance. For almost one thousand years, there were no renowned pulpit figures. While preaching did not cease altogether, it was in a general state of ineffectiveness which would continue until the Reformation.[11]

About three centuries prior to the Reformation, in 1215, the Fourth Lateran Council stimulated a renewal of proclamation. The church urged parish priests to preach in the vernacular and gave preaching in general more emphasis than it had received for centuries.

A more far-reaching impetus for renewal of preaching, however, began with the establishment of the preaching orders of Dominic (1170-1211) and Francis of Assissi (1182-1226), the former in France and the latter in Italy. Dominic and Francis both addressed in their sermons corruption in the church and the presence of heresy. The two orders demonstrated the importance of the pulpit. Their effectiveness in preaching served to advance both theory and practice of sermon building. The most brilliant and best known of the preaching friars was the Dominican, Thomas Aquinas (1225-1274).[12]

The preaching of John Wycliffe (ca. 1320-1384) fostered the reformation of preaching. An Englishman,

Wycliffe insisted that preaching was more important than the sacrament of the Eucharist. He trained his followers to preach simply so that the common people of England could understand the gospel. "Wycliffe became the mightiest champion of the new [recovered] doctrine of the primacy of preaching."[13]

Another prominent preacher who helped to prepare the way for the Reformation was Girolamo Savonarola (1452-1498) of Italy. His preaching, reminiscent of the Old Testament prophets, denounced social, political, and religious corruption.

Martin Luther (1483-1546), in his reforming zeal, rediscovered the power of the sermon in worship. A capable preacher, his study of Scripture led him to an emphasis on God's Word over the traditions of the Roman Catholic Church. Luther rejected the primacy of the Mass and replaced it with the authority of the Word of God brought to life in preaching. He sought to reform the liturgy, making the Word of God dominant. With his insistence that the sermon was central in worship, Luther put himself in direct opposition to Rome. His preaching and his criticism of the established church precipitated the Protestant Reformation.

Other preachers who pressed for church reform included John Calvin in Geneva (1509-1564), Huldreich Zwingli (1484-1531) in Vienna, John Knox in Scotland (1505-1572), and Thomas Crammer in England (1489-1556). To each, preaching was primary. Calvin, a prolific writer, left hundreds of biblical expositions in print. His commentaries on the Old and New Testaments are important even now for the study of preaching and theology.

*The Theological Basis of Preaching* **15**

The period of the Reformation and a hundred or so years following gave rise to the establishment of the major noncatholic church bodies throughout the world. The emphasis upon the congregational nature of the church and its worship advanced the preaching of the Word of God and affords the context within which proclamation ocurs in our century.

The accompanying decreasing emphasis on the sacraments soon vaulted preaching into the place of prominence which it presently holds in Protestantism. The reformers did not believe the Lord's Supper to be unimportant; they felt that the sacrament was incomplete without the preaching of the Word of God. The renewal and revival of preaching led to a recovery of the New Testament model of preaching with the proclamation of Jesus Christ as its central thrust.

### The Theological Significance of Preaching

The sermon spoken by the preacher, more than a simple statement of fact, confronts persons with the gospel and demands decisions from them. Since the gospel is news of a historical event with eternal significance, it is for every person. Genuine preaching occurs when the sermon closes the gap between God's Word and our situation.[14]

The preacher's responsibility to proclaim the message of Christ is one part of preaching. Another is people's need for the gospel. Humankind is in need of God since we were created for fellowship with Him. People hear the message from God through the preacher who faithfully tells them of Jesus who reconciles God and individuals.

The preacher must communicate with sinners in language and words that they can comprehend and, at the same time, the preacher must retain the content of the Bible in what he says. Thus, we will give attention to the preacher's task as interpreter and communicator in later chapters.

For the present, let us agree that the preacher, the hearer, and the message are alike involved in preaching. It is a complex matter. In a strange and wonderful way, God comes to persons through the sermon to redeem from sin. That is the very heart of theology and is the very heart of preaching. The preacher is a theologian whose task is greater than the mere statement and restatement of ideas: God uses him as an agent to bring persons and God, the Eternal and the Unseen, together through the words the preacher speaks (2 Cor. 5:18-19).

Preaching is an activity of the whole church. It is central to the life of the church since the church exists to proclaim the gospel. David H. C. Read has reminded us of the importance of the congregation's participation in the spoken Word when he has stressed the active involvement required in both speaking and hearing the Word.[15] This is the model found in New Testament proclamation when hearer response was phenomenal. The first event after the coming of the Spirit at Pentecost was a sermon. Peter stood up to proclaim that the startling developments of that day were the fulfillment of God's promises and purposes. The people gathered in a context of worship when the Spirit came and inspired vital listening and response as Peter preached the first sermon in the emerging church.

Preaching is an event expressive of Christ's coming in the flesh. The New Testament church declared that, in the totality of events from the birth of Christ through the resurrection, God had acted. Humanity rejected Christ and eventually crucified Him. On the third day after the crucifixion, God raised Christ from the dead. "He lives!" became the summary statement of the Christian message. The resurrection gave life and power to the gathered church. God's revelatory work accomplished in Christ became the message of the church giving new life through words to His life.

As the church grew, the word of God "increased" (Acts 6:7). Luke applied the metaphor of growth to God's word, implying the connection between church growth and preaching. The church neglects preaching, as a corporate responsibility, to its peril.

Preaching is a process by which the gospel becomes contemporaneous with those who hear—another part of the mystery of preaching. Christ confronts persons in today's world in the speaking of the gospel—a declaration of an event in time which has become timeless. Through the incarnation, eternity broke into time. In the recounting of that event, the preacher's words make the cross and resurrection contemporaneous with this generation. The eternal God confronts persons when the gospel is preached.

Preaching is a mystery pervaded by the presence of the Holy Spirit. Without His work in the preacher and the hearer, there can be no preaching. As the preacher does the work of interpreting the Scripture and preparing the sermon, the Spirit guides him. As he stands in the pulpit to deliver the message, the Spirit enables him.

Then, as the listener hears the sermon, the Spirit brings the Word to life. As the Spirit moved upon the body of the crucified Christ in the tomb, energized Him, and gave Him new life, so the Spirit moves in our human words, frail though they may be, and gives them life. In a manner similar to the Spirit's breathing on the church at Pentecost to give it the breath of life, so the Spirit breathes on our words as they enter human hearts. The words have power because of the transforming work of the Spirit.

Preaching is a call to faith and commitment. Proclamation brings about confrontation with the living, eternal Christ and *requires a decision*. This truth cannot be ignored or changed. We must acknowledge the claim of Christ on our lives or deny it to our peril. Acknowledgment in the form of a confession of faith leads to the commitment of life to Christ.

The preacher who proclaims the gospel is a partner with God in the issuing of a call to faith and commitment. "Come unto me" is the invitation of God made personal in Jesus Christ. Every sermon restates and reverberates the clarion call which God offers in invitation.

Preaching responds to Christ's command. When the Lord sent out the seventy (Luke 10:1 *ff.*), He instructed them to preach. Likewise, when He sent the twelve, He told them "to preach the kingdom of God" (Luke 9:2). Christ was an example in preaching. In addition, there is, as expressed by Paul, an inner compulsion to preach (2 Cor. 4:14). The divinely approved manner in which we make God's Christ known in our world is to go, stand and preach, to speak all the words of this life.

## Preaching in the Context of Worship

Indeed, contemporary churches maintain the prominence or newly regard the significance of the Word in worship. Preaching is God's addressing people. The other acts of worship are not insignificant, though some have assigned the sermon such importance as to diminish the impact of the music, prayer, and particularly, reading of Scripture.

Scripture, indeed, has a place in worship in and of itself. In some churches of the Reformed tradition, very little attention is given to the reading of Scripture. The principal reference to it occurs at the beginning of the sermon. In more liturgical traditions, the services of worship include reading an Old Testament lesson, a Gospel lesson and a selection from the Epistles.

A theology of preaching which gives place to the inherent power of the Word of God elevates Scripture to a position of prominence in the worship of the church. Through his Word, God addresses the worshiper. The service of the Word is significant. The preacher who holds this view of Scripture cannot believe that the only reason for reading a selection of verses is to lay down a platform from which the sermon springs. Neither can one who believes in the power of the Word itself read the verses carelessly, betraying little preparation for the Scripture reading, while demonstrating extensive preparation for the sermon. The exercise of such a choice whether conscious or unconscious is unfortunate.

Corporate worship is, itself, a form of proclamation. The church is the body of Christ. One cannot conduct a service of worship with all its components without proclaiming Christ. The service of worship provides the church an occasion for giving unanimous voice through music, praise, and sermon to the Word, the living Word of God. Our understanding of the theology of preaching elevates the public service of worship. When the church gathers for worship, once again the proclaimed becomes the proclaimer.[16]

The sermon as a living word recovers the element of celebration in worship. The early Christians in their sermons had one message: "He lives!" Their words were celebrations of the resurrection. The knowledge that words about Christ are made alive in the hearer again by the Holy Spirit gives the preacher cause for celebration in every sermon.

## Contemporary Relevance of Preaching

The Christian message is the ageless message of faith. It is a truth which abides as God's timeless word to people. God's breaking into time with His eternal Son remains pivotal for all people in all ages. When the preacher speaks God's word, he speaks a relevant word. The word of God does not have to be made relevant; it is relevant already. It waits only upon clear expression.

Yet the preacher faces the human difficulty of stating the ageless truth in the words of his age. In the contemporary world, that means speaking the word in a time of verbal inflation. Words are easy and cheap. Our generation is bombarded with words in a seemingly unending stream of information screaming for everyone's attention. Our technology enables us to record and retain all the information humanity possesses. Securing a hearing for the Word of God among all the words will

*The Theological Basis of Preaching*

be a growing challenge for preachers of this and following generations.

The preacher knows, however, that he has in his possession a word which modern people desperately need to hear. His proclamation is directed to the pressing personal needs of all who hear him. The one who speaks for God knows that he brings a message of hope, light, and life. He should remember that every time he stands to proclaim the word.

Above all, he should remember that he comes to God's people with God's Word. We proclaim the Christ of God, who is the same yesterday, today, and forever. The Christ of eternity and of the Scriptures stands before our listeners and confronts them as we bring words and the Spirit of God brings those words to life.

The word becomes flesh anew through preaching.

### Think on These Things

1. Refer to standard Bible dictionaries or concordances for definitions of the following: *word, prophet, preach, apostle, messenger,* and *gospel*.
2. Formulate your own definition of preaching.
3. Compare the status of preaching in contemporary times with its status in another period in history. How do you account for differences you perceive?
4. Find in the Bible sermons by Moses, Isaiah, Jeremiah, Amos, Jesus, Peter, and Paul. Study one of the sermons.
5. Survey the contemporary use of Scripture reading in services of worship.
6. Select a person introduced in the survey of the history of preaching about whom you would like to learn

more. Complete a biographical study of the one you select, emphasizing calling and preparation for ministry.
7. The preacher is often advised to be "relevant" in preaching. What is meant by that counsel? Are there cautions that we should observe as we seek a relevant word?

### Suggested Readings

Armstrong, James. *Telling Truth: The Foolishness of Preaching in a Real World.* Waco, Tex.: Word Books, Publisher, 1977.

Brilioth, Yngve. *A Brief History of Preaching.* Translated by Karl E. Mattson. Philadelphia: Fortress Press, 1965.

Daane, James. *Preaching with Confidence: A Theological Essay on the Power of the Pulpit.* Grand Rapids: William B. Eerdmans Publishing Company, 1980.

Fant, Clyde E., Jr. and Pinson, William M., Jr., eds. *20 Centuries of Great Preaching.* 13 vols. Waco, Tex.: Word Book Publishers, 1971.

Farmer, Herbert H. *The Servant of the Word.* Philadelphia: Fortress Press, 1942.

Ford, D. W. Cleverley. *The Ministry of the Word.* Great Britain: William B. Eerdmans Publishing Company, 1979.

Forsyth, P. T. *Positive Preaching and The Modern Mind.* New York: Hodder and Stoughton, 1907.

Holland, Dewitte, ed. *Preaching in American History.* Nashville: Abingdon Press, 1969.

Kennedy, Gerald. *His Word Through Preaching.* New York: Harper & Brothers Publishers, 1947.

Lloyd-Jones, D. Martyn. *Preaching and Preachers.* Grand Rapids: Zondervan Publishing House, 1971.
Miller, Donald G. *Fire in Thy Mouth.* Nashville: Abingdon, 1954.
Rust, Eric C. *The Word and Words.* Macon, Ga.: Mercer University Press, 1982.
Scherer, Paul. *The Word God Sent.* New York: Harper & Row, Publishers, 1965.
Turnbull, Ralph G. *A History of Preaching.* 3. Grand Rapids: Baker Book House, 1974.

### Notes

1. A conviction expressed also by John R. W. Stott in *Between Two Worlds: The Art of Preaching in the Twentieth Century* (Grand Rapids: William B. Eerdmans Publishing Company, 1982), p. 10.
2. Edmund P. Clowney, *Preaching and Biblical Theology* (Phillipsburg, N.J.: Presbyterian and Reformed Publishing Co., 1979), p. 45.
3. See Clowney, ibid., and Richard Lischer, *A Theology of Preaching: The Dynamics of the Gospel,* Abingdon Preacher's Library, ed. William D. Thompson (Nashville: Abingdon, 1981). Clyde E. Fant, *Preaching for Today* (New York: Harper & Row, 1975), pp. 19-27 has an excellent summary of the views on preaching held by major theologians.
4. Donald Miller calls preaching a redemptive deed. See *Fire in Thy Mouth* (Nashville: Abingdon Press, 1954), pp. 13-36. David H. C. Read says preaching is a sacrament. See *Sent From God: The Enduring Power and Mystery of the Gospel* (Nashville: Abingdon Press, 1974), pp. 14; 30-43.
5. A good review of the New Testament words translated "preach" is found in H. C. Brown, Jr.; H. Gordon Clinard; and Jesse J. Northcutt, *Steps to the Sermon: A Plan for Sermon Preparation* (Nashville: Broadman Press, 1963), pp. 4-8.
6. Clowney, *Preaching and Biblical Theology,* p. 49.
7. Ibid., p. 43.
8. James Daane, *Preaching with Confidence: A Theological Essay on the Power of the Pulpit* (Grand Rapids: William B. Eerdmans Publishing Company, 1980), p. 48.
9. See Edwin C. Dargan, *A History of Preaching,* Introduction by J. B. Weatherspoon, 2 vols. (New York: George H. Doran Co., 1905; reprint ed., Grand Rapids: Baker Book House, 1968). These volumes are the sources for this summary of the history of preaching.

10. T. DeWitte Holland, *The Preaching Tradition: A Brief History*, The Abingdon Preacher's Library, ed. William D. Thompson (Nashville: Abingdon, 1980), p. 28.
11. Ibid., p. 35.
12. Ibid., p. 39.
13. Ibid., p. 40
14. Fant, *Preaching for Today*, p. 107.
15. Read, *Sent from God*, p. 12.
16. Lischer, *A Theology of Preaching*, p. 73.

# 2

# The Personal Basis of Preaching

Preaching is inseparable from the preacher. While it is true that the power resides in the Word, it also is true that the human instrument affects the proclamation of the message significantly. The personal basis of preaching is vital to a proper understanding of preaching. We must ask the question: Who is the preacher? The answer gives the preacher an identity and instills a sense of confidence within him.

## The Principal Prerequisite: Faith

He who asks others to have faith and live by that faith must possess it himself. The preacher's basic message calls for faith in God through Jesus Christ. Remarkably, the God who requires us to have faith gives us the ability to exercise that very faith. Each person responds to the inner working of the Spirit and thereby comes to life. The preacher, the herald of the good news, makes a response to this gift of faith. This most obvious fact must never be taken for granted by the preacher or his congregation.

Once in the faith, Christians assume responsibility to grow in that faith. The context in which they do that is the congregation—the local church. Our Lord "increased in wisdom and in stature, and in favor with God and man" (Luke 2:52), thereby revealing his identity with humanity and God. Also, he attended the synagogue regularly (Luke 4:16).

The minister, or preacher, is often the most overlooked member of the church. Because of his role as the leader of the church and its ministry, he forgets that he also is a member of the congregation (a fact some church members either do not know or ignore).

His role as the shepherd of the flock, with its attendant responsibility as the provider of food (Acts 20:28; 1 Pet. 4:1-4), does not exempt him from the need to be fed himself. He is a learner. He depends on the congregation for his personal growth. As Willard F. Jabusch observes, "We grow with our people. . . . Preachers need people."[1] There is no way one can teach all the time and never need teaching. How is it that a minister can feel so at home as one among sinners prior to conversion but ill at ease as a Christian among Christians following his conversion?

Congregations, as well as pastors, need reminding that the preacher depends upon his members for his spiritual nourishment. They support, sustain, and encourage him, as well as provide him an assembled body for the Sunday sermons. He needs their love and must love them in return.

Pastors easily can overlook this need to grow within the context of the community of faith. Yet the preacher's faith, like that of his members, cannot grow as it should when he is isolated. He who always is giving and never receiving soon will have depleted his store.

Practically, this means the preacher (minister/pastor) must make a personal commitment to maturing in the life of the faith. The preacher is a learner all of his life. Should he need reminders for growing in commitment, let him remember his conversation and his response to the call for ministry. Both require a continuing response, as well as an initial commitment. Wallace Fisher describes the growth of the Christian as "disciplined response to God's Word."[2]

We ministers are fellow strugglers with all Christians in the matter of personal growth. "If we who preach understand our own need to grow as Christians in an ongoing conversion of mind and heart, then we will be able to respond to the religious needs of the people we care for."[3] We do not have to experience everything they do, but we must see the world and walk into it to minister to those who are there. We should recall, often, that one of the temptations we face is that of handling the contents of the faith only long enough to pass them along to others. In that way, the holy may become commonplace; the extraordinary, ordinary. Just as no doctor would prescribe medicine he would not take for the same ailment, the minister should not dispense a gospel which he would not live by or recommend to others something he would not do.

An immature person is incapable of assisting others toward maturity. The preacher should learn to be interdependent on others in the fellowship of faith and to draw support from them. As he leads in prayer, let him pray. As he leads in worship, let him worship. As he teaches, let him receive his own teaching.

This may mean for the pastor an occasional visit to the Sunday School classroom of an adult Bible class. Also, it may mean that he will sit and listen attentively when guest ministers instruct the congregation.

For the congregation, it may mean that they will expect their pastor to sit with them as a participant in worship now and then and will not feel that, in so doing, he is neglecting his duty or taking time off. The pastor is never off duty while present with his people. That is the nature of his existence. The membership should know and remember that the pastor may be the only church member without a pastor.

To be sure, the preacher gains knowledge and food for growth as he does his private study (as any other person should do), but there are times when he needs the privilege of group worship. He cannot always do that while on vacation. Even if he could, he would not be with his own people.

Pastors have obligations to their flocks. That seems perfectly understood by most church members. On the other hand, they, as Christians, have some obligations to him—not as a pastor—but as a fellow Christian.

### Set Apart for Good Work—The Call to Service

The call to preach leads to service. The one called prepares, formally or informally, then seeks a place to serve. That place usually is the local church pastorate. Churches call pastors and expect them to perform a multitude of duties, the most important of which is to preach. From the time he first accepts the invitation to become pastor, the minister assumes two identities in one office: pastor and preacher. He sets a tension in his ministry that remains throughout his tenure of service. His vocation is to serve faithfully, fulfilling both functions of ministry.

The image of the minister as a professional is a new

## The Personal Basis of Preaching

concept given to us by a modern, technological culture. It revolves around the concepts of competence and practical techniques of management of oneself and others. Fisher dismisses such imagery as inadequate to describe the minister.[4] The minister should not let culture dictate his role. If he accepts any other concept outside the scriptural one, he may succeed; but in doing so, he will sacrifice the true meaning of his person and his ministry.

Every minister should have a high level of competency, integrity, and ability; but he should not allow business standards of operation, management, and success to control his understanding of ministry.

The word *minister* is both a verb and a noun. Jesus did not refer to himself as a minister, in the professional sense, but he did say, "The Son of man came not to be ministered unto, but *to minister*" (Mark 10:45, KJV, authors' italics). He envisioned himself as the embodiment of the servant image in the Old Testament (principally Isa. 52:13 to 53:12). Jesus came to serve. The church's mission today is to continue that servant role in the world. The pastor/preacher is the minister responsible for leading the church in ministry.

On the other hand, Paul described himself as *a minister*. He had in mind one who served the risen Lord. Paul referred to himself often as a servant, a slave for Jesus Christ. His understanding of his role was that he should serve others humbly in the spirit of his Lord. He never had in mind the image of a "professional person" with clearly defined duties to perform.

The testimony of most ministers is that we received the call to ministry while in the context of the church, the community of faith. Whether that is true or not, the call to serve is a call to serve in a community. Generally, ordination does not occur until after a specific invitation to serve in a church context. In a sense, the church validates the call—confirms the commitment. In some traditions, the call is tested by the church or representatives of the church. The community is the place where the gifts for ministry are developed and recognized. Generally, in response to our public declaration of an inward sense of call, the congregations take specific action to separate ministers for service. The ceremonial setting apart for ministry is ordination.

The biblical precedent for the call is clear. Each prophet spoke of the Lord's initiating contact with him which resulted in a commitment to ministry. The New Testament apostles, especially Paul, recount similar confrontation. What more dramatic call is there in all of the New Testament than the experience of Saul of Tarsus on the road to Damascus?

Likewise, the response of the New Testament church when one gives evidence of a call is clear. Acts 13:1 reveals that the church set Paul and Barnabas apart for ministry. It is the responsibility of the church to help the candidate evaluate and understand the call to ministry. As Fisher reminds us: "In-depth dialogues with each candidate about the nature and purpose of biblical ministry—and his or her personal call—are a pressing need in the church today."[5] The church must question the candidates for ministry to be certain of their call and commitment.

One further word about the minister's call and the church he will serve. The pastor of a modern church

*The Personal Basis of Preaching*

cannot be a specialist. He must embody all the images of ministry—priest, prophet, teacher. Yes, it is a full-time job, but he cannot *do* all the ministry; he must lead his people to an understanding of their roles as ministers who assist one another with the performance of the church's tasks of worship, service, and witness (1 Pet. 4:1-4).

## The Cultivation of Knowledge

That a minister of the gospel possesses knowledge is a given. He knows the risen Christ and should desire to know more about Him. He knows the essentials of the body of faith which is the heritage of his church and tradition. He knows his congregation and senses their specific requirements for growth.

The minister's knowledge is never complete. The faith which he possesses is an ever-expanding body of knowledge. The metaphor of Colossians 2:6-7, "rooted and built up in him," suggests growth in the faith. The more one understands about one's faith the more one realizes what he does not yet know.

We gain knowledge of the essentials of the faith from a continuing study of Scripture, the history of biblical interpretation, theology, and our tradition. In short, the minister must give attention to the content of the faith. He will discover that its acquisition is a lifetime process. Even a learned man like the apostle Paul declared: "I do not consider that I have made it my own" (Phil. 3:13). That declaration suggests the importance of the continuing nature of the Christian's growth.

The Christian faith, however, is not merely information to be learned. Faith must be experienced to become personal. Knowledge for the sake of knowledge, in other words, is inadequate for the Christian. Information gained through experience is a pearl of great price—a priceless treasure. When Paul asserted, "I decided to know nothing among you except Jesus Christ and him crucified" (1 Cor. 2:2), he was not suggesting there is only one sermon in the preacher's file. He affirmed that he preached a Christ he *knew*.

The desire to know the matters of faith should carry with it a commensurate yearning to learn to love God with the whole mind. When the inquisitive lawyer asked Jesus which was the greatest commandment, he precipitated a discussion about man's loving God with the totality of his being. In his response, Jesus clarified that the whole person is involved in salvation. "You shall love the Lord your God with all your heart, and with all your soul, and with all your mind" (Matt. 22:37). Learning to love God with the whole mind is no option for the Christian. If the preacher needs justification for his educational pursuits, he has it in this admonition from Jesus.

The human mind is a marvel with its incredible capacity for information. A preacher who wishes to devote his whole mind to God has cut a broad path for himself. Yet, he can do no less. The minister is not in the task alone. The Holy Spirit is his teacher. Before Jesus ascended to the Father he promised to send the Spirit. "When [he] . . . comes, he will guide you into all the truth." He was saying in effect: He will be your teacher—as I was your teacher. He will be another comforter—another of the same kind (see John 14:16; 16:13-14).

In all our study and preparation for preaching, preachers must never presume upon the work of the Spirit. He is our guide as we seek understanding of the Word and the faith. Without him we would be mere humans addressing other humans in human words. With him our words have life and power.

One of the greatest temptations for the minister is to do all of his work in sermon preparation and then presume that it will succeed because he has taken all the steps, has not skimped at any point, has constructed his sermon as he was taught to do. In fact, he feels great pressure (both from within and from without) to succeed. Our success-oriented culture, with its "how-to" books and programs, requires that he succeed. Therefore, he stands over a carefully prepared manuscript, written with great care and precision, and commands it to live.

Alas, how simple preaching would be if sermon preparation and preaching were that simple. The wise preacher remembers, though, that only God's Spirit can bring to life the words written on a page and spoken by the human instrument. The Spirit enables the preacher to learn and empowers him to speak.

## Personal Commitment to the Gospel and Its Demands

Few Christians know the demands of the gospel better than the preacher. It is sad but true that preachers sometimes make demands on the people in the name of the gospel more effectively than we press home to the people the demands of the gospel. There is a great difference between the two kinds of demands. The wise preacher who knows the difference may easily forget that he lives by the gospel he preaches.

Another way of stating the issue is that the preacher should know by experience what he professes. Great pronouncements about the strength of the Lord are just that, pronouncements, until they are a part of the life of the preacher. That applies to more than the subject of one's salvation. Faith in God brings sustaining power to the Christian. Even God's children will experience difficulty on occasion, and we all must know by experience that our faith will see us through every valley, as well as carry us to the top of the mountain. The preacher should say only what he knows to be true. His own trust in God will likely come through as he encourages others to trust in the Father.

Moreover, the preacher must demonstrate that he meets the demands of personal and social justice required in Scripture. One standard for the minister and another for his congregation will hamper the advance of Christianity and weaken the appeal of the gospel. Willard Jabusch reminds us that the people want us to be holy,[6] though every minister knows how difficult that is!

One of the most serious problems faced by the Old Testament prophet Jeremiah was the failure of some prophets to measure up to the requirements of God's law. The false prophets described in Jeremiah 23 lived as though there would be no judgment and encouraged others to live the same way. Their deceit and treachery set a poor example for the Israelites.

Another of the great temptations for the minister is to believe that "right living" is what he tells others to do; it is not something he practices himself. The minister must be a person of basic piety and integrity. He recommends the life of faith to others because he lives it himself. He shares the gospel because of a compulsion to recommend what has made him a new person. We must not neglect our own spiritual walk and growth.

This commitment to Christ supports the inner compulsion to preach. "The love of Christ controls us," declared Paul (2 Cor. 5:14). This control or constraint is a dynamic force at work within the heart. If the personal commitment of the preacher has led him to a deeper understanding of faith, a call to greater service, the hunger for an expanding knowledge, and a response to the demands of God and his Word, who can but preach? A commitment which revolutionizes and remakes life is worth sharing. The bones burn to tell (Jer. 20:9); the mouth is filled with words to speak (Jer. 1:9).

We speak what we have heard and tell what we have felt. This progression naturally leads to the involvement of other people. Such speaking and telling warrants and receives a hearing from those whose experience is similar and from those who sense a need as yet unfulfilled by their experience.

## Discovering and Developing Skills for Proclaiming the Gospel

Involvement with other people immediately makes the task of the minister a complex one. To tell, he must have someone to listen; to share, he must have someone with whom to relate. Since the gospel is more than information, the proclamation of the gospel is more than the transfer of information. The minister must develop a variety of skills in human communication if he is to minister the Word to hearers in response to his inner compulsion to preach.

One of the most basic skills, warmly relating to people, is no simple matter. To relate properly, the minister must learn to understand people—knowing their likes and dislikes, their abilities or limitations, their favorable responses, and those things which offend them. The preacher who cannot relate to persons warmly has a difficult, if not impossible, ministry ahead of him.

A significant factor in relating to others is to grant them worth and identity. The lack of self-worth, the feeling of worthlessness, is a common problem in the hectic pace of a busy world. The minister must learn to affirm a person and, at the same time, help that person to understand his need for the new birth and the attendant change in character. The minister must see in everyone a somebody with potential to grow into the image of Christ.

The preacher deceives himself if he believes he can ignore or fail to relate to his people throughout the week and then, on Sunday morning, apply the balm of Gilead to their wounds. The people want to feel that he knows who they are, that he cares about them as individuals, and that he relates to them fully. The minister cannot afford the luxury of insensitivity. He must relate to each individual as a person, a companion down life's highway.

This matter of relating goes beyond the pastor's ability as a counselor to include his informal, nonstructured contacts with the people who sit before him when he preaches. His attitude toward them and his ability to

## The Personal Basis of Preaching

relate to them in the marketplace, at the high-school basketball games, or at the kitchen table with a hot cup of coffee will be evident in his manner and in his speech. Pastoral work is a valuable resource for learning to relate to others. "A preacher who cannot because of emotional instability, or will not because of temperamental disability, relate in depth to people will not become a biblical preacher."[7] One who loves God will love God's people. Relating to people requires an openness and an honesty on the part of the preacher. He cannot be fearful and insecure. To be open and honest, the minister must be healthy in mind and spirit.

We preachers are involved with the Word and with people. We must learn to relate properly to each—to keep in touch with people in order to communicate with them and with the Scriptures in order to have something to say.

A second necessity for proclaiming the gospel is development of communicative skills and verbal skills. When the Athenians saw Paul in the marketplace, they asked themselves, "What would this babbler say?" (Acts 17:18). They meant those words as an insult, implying that he would mumble incoherently for a while and add nothing to their learning. The preacher who fails to develop his verbal skills may have the people asking—*after* he speaks—"What did this babbler say?" That comment would be an affront to the gospel he preaches.

While the power resides in the Word, the power of expression resides in the minister. Remember: the mystery of preaching is that God uses our human words to express his divine Word. We are more than conduits; we are conductors, carriers of the Word. The meaning of the gospel may fail to come through if we fail to express it clearly.

The preacher must learn to communicate the gospel as clearly as possible. For that, he depends both upon communicative skills and verbal skills. The power of expression is vital to the minister. He develops it with practice. To test your expressive capabilities, state the simple truth, "God is love," in as many ways as you can. Be sure that in each you retain the original meaning of this beautiful declaration. Now attempt something more complex: "For I am not ashamed of the gospel: it is the power of God for salvation" (Rom. 1:16). Our expressive ability must be compatible with the verbal force of the Scriptures we employ. Thus, the development of verbal skills is imperative.

Yet another requirement for proclamation is the development of receptive skills. It is the nature of people, as individuals and collectively, to send signals to a speaker who stands before them. This means that the preacher must have the skills to receive and interpret the signals.

While we preach, giving attention to what we say and to how our words are being received is not an easy matter. When we sit across from an individual in a counseling session, we can read response and make suitable adjustments. But reading feedback one to many in the preaching situation is much more difficult.

A basic identification with people is the beginning point for acquiring the skills of receptivity. The preacher must know his people to be able to understand their responses. If he has this knowledge, he creates a bond between himself and his listeners and can sense what

## The Personal Basis of Preaching

they say to him as he communicates a message to them. Their facial expressions, motions, and general demeanor all serve as signals to the perceptive preacher.

Gary Stratman in his excellent book on pastoral preaching[8] stresses that listening to people in the pastoral context will enable the preacher to be more effective in the pulpit. The pastor, in his role as a counselor, acquires and develops his receptive skills.

A fourth necessity for proclaiming the gospel is the development of evaluative skills. Evaluation carries no automatic negative connotation. The development of critical skills will enable the minister to evaluate his effectiveness. Their use will enable him to discern in others characteristics to emulate or eliminate from his preaching or approach to ministry.

The preacher should begin by evaluating himself. To do so, let him ask himself a series of questions. What do I make of my call? How does the call to serve motivate me to preach? What kinds of talents do I possess? What is important to me? Where are my strong points, and in what ways am I weak? The practice of beginning with self will keep the minister from developing a judgmental spirit.

Evaluation serves the purpose of discovering facts about oneself. Once he deals honestly with his own motives, interests, and responses, the preacher is better prepared to apply the tests to others.

The preacher should know that the response of the listener is both to the message content and to the messenger. In this complex matter of human communication, no one element of the process can be considered in isolation. Indeed, our consideration of the personal basis of preaching anticipates dimensions of the processes of communication which shall be discussed in more detail in other chapters. But the focus here is upon the personal basis of preaching identified as faith, call, responsiveness to the gospel's claim and its proclamation.

The Roman rhetorician Quintilian defined the orator as a "good man, speaking well." Indeed, the gospel states a requirement no less exacting: the preacher must be a good person; he must speak well.

## Think on These Things

1. Compose a spiritual autobiography emphasizing your sense of call to ministry and response. To what extent was the fellowship of Christians supportive of your decision? Particular individuals?
2. Plan an ordination service designed to set apart the candidate for ministry. If you have been ordained, compare your service to that which you deem to be meaningful presently.
3. Suggest specific ways the church can help its pastor develop full potential. How may the church be led to meet the responsibility to nurture the minister?
4. Formulate a plan for your personal growth as a Christian and as a minister for the year upcoming.
5. Do a word study employing standard reference tools for each of the following: *disciple, minister, pastor, ordain,* and *church.*

## Suggested Readings

Hiltner, Seward. *The Christian Shepherd: Some Aspects of Pastoral Care.* Nashville: Abingdon Press, 1959.

Hobbs, Herschel H. *Preacher Talk*. Nashville: Broadman Press, 1979.

McEachern, Alton H. *Set Apart for Service: Baptist Ordination Practices*. Nashville: Broadman Press, 1980.

Oates, Wayne E. *The Christian Pastor*. Philadelphia: The Westminster Press, 1951.

Robertson, A. T. *Types of Preachers in the New Testament*. Grand Rapids: Baker Book House, 1972.

Scherer, Paul. *For We Have This Treasure*. Lyman Beecher Lectures, Yale University. New York: Harper & Row, Publisher, 1943.

Switzer, David K. *Pastor, Preacher, Person: Developing a Pastoral Ministry in Depth*. Nashville: Abingdon Press, 1979.

Turnbull, Ralph G. *The Preacher's Heritage, Task, and Resources*. Grand Rapids: Baker Book House, 1968.

Willimon, William H. *Integrative Preaching: The Pulpit at the Center*. Abingdon Preacher's Library, ed. William D. Thompson. Nashville: Abingdon Press, 1981.

### Notes

1. Willard F. Jabusch, *The Person in the Pulpit: Preaching as Caring*, The Abingdon Preacher's Library, ed. William D. Thompson (Nashville: Abingdon, 1980), p. 58.
2. Wallace E. Fisher, *Who Dares to Preach? The Challenge of Biblical Preaching* (Minneapolis: Augsburg Publishing House, 1979), pp. 76, 82.
3. Jabusch, p. 59.
4. Fisher, pp. 61-62.
5. Ibid., p. 60.
6. Jabusch, p. 91.
7. Fisher, p. 100.
8. Gary Stratman, *Pastoral Preaching: Timeless Truth for Changing Needs* (Nashville: Abingdon Press, 1983), pp. 40-44.

# 3

# The Social Basis of Preaching

In the Protestant tradition, preaching occurs in corporate worship in a body composed of the fellowship of believers. The community of faith gathers for the purpose of worshiping God. The relatedness inherent in worship has a vertical dimension facilitating communication from God to us as well as from us to God. There is also the horizontal dimension of worship—the interaction of person to person.

Evelyn Underhill asserts that worship is social. Further she affirms that solitary worship is impossible because the individual engages in communication through prayer and praise with God who draws near to the worshiper.[1] By definition corporate worship is social. Corporate means *persons united*. The congregating body, the gathered church united for worship, includes believers all of whom actively engage in the elements of the service.

## Worship as Communication

In worship, persons gather with other believers to participate in the elements which speak anew the Word of grace: the primarily verbal acts of prayer, praise, proclamation, invitation, and response, and the real and symbolic acts of personal faith, giving, touching, baptism, and the Lord's Supper. *Prayer* is all addressed to God. *Praise* encompasses the devotional elements in corporate worship. *Proclamation, invitation,* and *response* include the speaking of the word of Scripture and the words of the sermon, the extending of the invitation to faith and to deepened maturity in faith, and the response of all worshipers. The *actual* events of giving and touching augment the *symbolic* nature of the ordinances of baptism and the Lord's Supper.

We participate with other believers in the *elements which speak anew the Word of grace.* Prominent among these elements is the act of proclamation of the gospel in the sermon. Our definition asserts that in this element, as in the others, the congregation is active: The speaker and the hearers of the gospel are *participants.* Preaching is, then, social, interpersonal, and directed toward hearer response.

A congregation composed of persons who actively listen supports the effectiveness of the Word preached. There is encouragement and reinforcement in positive listening behavior which facilitates the preacher's task as proclaimer. Active listening becomes pervasive as individual encourages individual through expectation and realization: God will speak; God has spoken, and through response continually and ultimately, during the service, at the climax of invitation, and beyond.

The communications model for proclamation (chart 1) indicates the process of message formation, presentation, reception, and response. The cycle of communication in preaching (chart 2) graphically demonstrates the

## Chart 1
## A Communications Model for Proclamation

MESSAGE      (discovered in the biblical text; relevant to the needs of the fellowship of believers individually and collectively; born in prayer; nurtured through the Holy Spirit; claiming the preacher as believer; claimed by the preacher for other believers)

ENCODING      (as Scripture through the text; as verbal act through development, support, structure, and expression)

PREACHING AS WORD SPOKEN      (verbal and nonverbal message transmission; voice, action, attitude)

DECODING      (hearer reconstructs and responds to the text; interprets the message in terms of individual and collective needs; discovers enlightenment through the Holy Spirit; perceives the verbal signals in terms of support, structure, and expression, the nonverbal signals of action and attitude)

MESSAGE RESPONSE      (comprehension based upon decoding transmitted signals; degree of correspondence with preacher's intended message indication of effectiveness; immediate or ultimate change)

## Chart 2
## The Cycle of Communication in Preaching

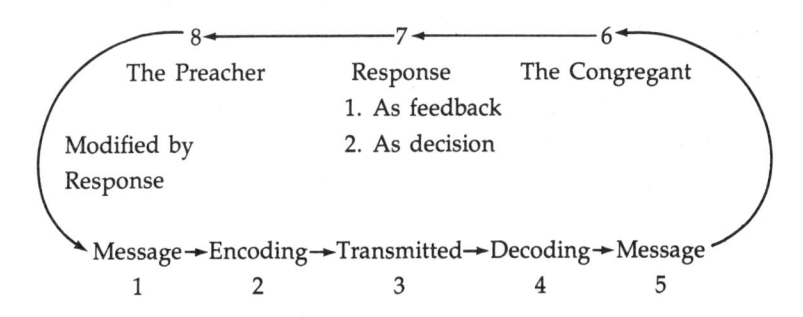

```
    ┌──── 8 ←─────────── 7 ←─────────── 6 ←────┐
    │  The Preacher      Response      The Congregant │
    │                    1. As feedback                │
    │  Modified by       2. As decision                │
    │  Response                                        │
    └→ Message → Encoding → Transmitted → Decoding → Message ┘
         1          2           3            4          5
```

result of response as feedback and as decision. Let us explore the interpersonal dimensions of the process through an examination of the stages of the communicative act.

**Message**

An idea born in the mind of the preacher is the genesis of the message. The idea occurs at a point of intersection between the minister's consciousness of personal and corporate need within the congregation he serves and the Scripture. Ideally the intersection occurs as the preacher hears the Word and recognizes its relevance as he studies systematically for sermon preparation or as he meditates upon the Word devotionally. He grasps the significance of the Word in the light of his consciousness of need. The reverse is possible as well. The minister discovers need as topics which require attention from the Scriptures read and explicated through proclamation.

Prayer for guidance of the Holy Spirit and serious study merge into a stream of development which seeks a channel of sufficient depth to contain the message. An occasional tributary will be explored then abandoned as the search continues. As the thought emerges, the message develops. It claims the preacher. It speaks to his deep need, and he hears and responds. He claims that Word for his hearers whose needs guide its development.

**Encoding**

The message must become transmittable: Verbal and nonverbal signals must be selected. Intentionality prevails. The preacher crafts content, support, structure, and expression. He frames principal concepts, selects supporting materials, arranges the components of the message, seeks clarity and beauty in their statement. *Encoding* involves selecting expressions that are faithful to the requirements of the Word to be spoken and which are capable of being understood by those who listen.

**Preaching or Transmission**

The encoded message is transmitted by the preacher employing voice and action. The stimuli originating with the preacher are only a part of those present in the message environment. There are other sounds and sights within the hearers' field of consciousness. These competing, disorganized signals must be overcome by the preacher's communicative skill: vocal energy and physical involvement.

Since the message environment is a worship service, the focus of those assembled will be fixed upon the message-source, the preacher, when he begins the message. Competing signals will be ignored or filtered out initially because the worshiper has voluntarily attended a service where a message is an integral component of the series of expected events. If, however, the hearer is unaccustomed to the conventions of worship, such openness to the message may not be granted but must be won. Even when the worshiper accustomed to the preaching dimension of the service extends openness to the message-source, preservation of that attitude depends upon the preacher's capability to get the message across.

The environment may reduce the impact of competing stimuli by the placement of the pulpit and by amplification of the preacher's voice. Nevertheless, the transmission effectiveness is contingent upon the clarity of the verbal signals and the complementary visual impact of gesture, directness of eye contact, and movement. These nonverbal signals are indications of the preacher's physical involvement with his message. The fact that the environment includes competing elements which distract attention *(noise)* supports the necessity of the preacher's utilization of communicative skills to gain and hold the attention of the congregation through dominance in the environment of his *signals*, the spoken word.

An attitude which reinforces the presentation is an essential component of message transmission. The hearer perceives the preacher's responsiveness to the claim of the message upon his life and his earnestness in commending, as well, the claim upon the hearers' lives. He honors the text. He looks to the Holy Spirit to enliven his representation of the impact of the text upon his life and upon the lives of the hearers. That attitude kindles an intensity of utterance and involvement essential to effectiveness in message transmission.

**Decoding the Message**

The transmitted message must be decoded by the hearers. The verbal and nonverbal signals must be received and assigned meaning. Hearers reconstruct the message based upon their interpretation of the verbal and nonverbal indicators of meaning transmitted by the preacher.

A common language (perception of structure and vocabulary) facilitates faithful reconstruction of the message in the consciousness of those listening to the message. Skills in listening aid the hearers. Breadth of experience and awareness of personal needs enable the hearer not only to attend to the Word preached but to apprehend the Word through a recognition of its worth and its pointedness in answering specific life needs. When the message apprehended by the hearer corresponds exactly with the message transmitted by the preacher, the communication process has been maximally effective. While that degree of effectiveness may not be achieved, it shapes the assessment of effectiveness as the standard sought.

An indication of the spiritual dimension of the preaching task emerges, however, when the experience in faith or consciousness of personal need combines with the message spoken to communicate the Word in a profoundly moving way to an individual hearer. The impact of the message may exceed that of the words encoded and the transmission in speech and action to become the living Word among the hearers leading to personal commitment.

## Response

The interpersonal nature of the communicative process in preaching becomes apparent in the recognition that we preach in anticipation of response. The response may be immediate feedback, indicators of comprehension, agreement, and recognition of message applicability or their opposites. A look of understanding, a nod of agreement, and an urgent interest communicate to the preacher a reinforcement of the sermon content and presentation. Feedback as puzzlement, shaking the head no, or apparent disinterest requires the preacher's modification of the message to offer clearer explanation, to defuse disagreement by restatement with compelling support from Scriptures or from acknowledged authorities, or to enliven the presentation by directly applicable illustration.

Again, response may be immediate or long term, the message immediately or ultimately effective. The environment of worship may be viewed by the preacher as conducive to immediate response. In a worship tradition which encompasses the verbal acts of *proclamation, invitation, and response,* an immediate indicator of message effectiveness in public decision is present. Ultimate response indicated through changed perspectives, life-style modification, Christian action, or improved relationships present greater difficulty when we seek to measure them. The spiritual health of the congregation and the maturity in Christ characteristic of the members while subjectively assessed, may at the same time offer the strongest indications of the ongoing and cumulative strength of the preaching ministry of the church.

## The Cycle of Communication

$$M_1 \longrightarrow M_2 \longrightarrow M_3 \longrightarrow M_1$$

The cycle of communication describes message transmission, reception, modification, and reinforcement, as follows:

$M_1$ the Message as understood by the preacher and transmitted with a degree of communication skill

$M_2$ the Message as understood by the hearer; accurate reception contingent upon the degree of communication skill in the message source and the listening skills, interest, and experience of the hearer; reception accompanied by feedback

$M_3$ the preacher reads the feedback and accordingly modifies his Message

$M_1$ the hearer moves closer toward reception of the original Message; positive feedback reinforces the preacher's presentation

The preacher may sense response as negative feedback or as a failure on the part of the hearer to focus upon the message among the competing stimuli in the preaching environment. Message modification is essential in either event.

The chief value of our examination of preaching from the perspective of a communications model[2] is that we find fresh approaches to the understanding of our task and of the interpersonal and social dimensions of the experience. The framework we employ in this way may reveal few if any new insights. It affords, however, the means for reexamination of our procedures and serves as a vehicle for discovering anew the cooperative enterprise that is the speaking and hearing of the gospel.

## Characteristics of Listeners

The Christian faith recognizes that both the preacher and the hearer are vital to preaching. Romans 10:14 and 17 establish this principle:

> But how are men to call upon him in whom they have not believed? And how are they to believe in him of whom they have never heard? And how are they to hear without a preacher? So faith comes from what is heard, and what is heard comes by the preaching of Christ.

A threefold pattern emerges:
1. The *preacher* preaches Christ.
2. The *hearer* listens to the preaching.
3. The hearer responds in *faith*.

James 1:22; "Be ye doers of the world, and not hearers only," may be understood, "Don't listen, do!" That misreading of the text typifies many who haven't listened to the gospel in years and who will not as long as action may be substituted for listening. If any activity consistently results in persons' failing to hear the Word proclaimed, even if that activity is a worthwhile, church-oriented task, it needs to be reevaluated in keeping with the priority activity of the corporate body: hearing the preaching of Christ. James reminded us that our right action emanates from hearing: *Do* as well as *hear*—be *doers* as well as *hearers*.

Further, Paul admonished in Ephesians 4, "Let everyone speak the truth" (v. 25), advice applicable to all Christians but equally essential for the preacher. Paul continued, "Let no evil talk come out of your mouths, but only such [talk] as is good for edifying, as fits the occasion, that it [your talk] may impart grace to those who hear" (v. 29). The spoken word must build up, be suitable, and impart grace. The hearer must accept edification, hear the message as applicable, and receive grace as the gospel is spoken. Our preaching corresponds for our age with that of the disciples for theirs. Of their preaching, Jesus said, "He who hears you hears me" (Luke 10:16). Implicit in Jesus' statement is the expectation of hearing the message which points to Christ. That is certainly the sense of Matthew 13:9, "Let him who has ears listen!" (Williams).

David H. C. Read reminds us that pulpits on the preacher side frequently carry the scriptural expectation, "Sir, we would see Jesus" (John 12:21, KJV). He observes that the people side of the pulpit should speak for the congregation, "Speak, Lord, for thy servant hears" (1 Sam. 3:9).[3] Faithful preaching is to be met with faithful hearing. The agent of grace is the spoken Word capable through the Spirit of imparting the love of Christ both to the preacher and to the hearer.

### Listening

Among the verbal tasks which occupy our waking hours, the typical adult spends more time listening than in any of the other three: writing, reading, and speaking.

## The Social Basis of Preaching

Since we are engaged in listening so much of the time, it is notable that little attention is given to the development of listening skills in programs of education. The definition of worship discussed previously recognized the importance of the gathered congregation as participants in the elements which speak anew the Word of grace: The goal is for those who gather, the *congregation*, to become those who listen, the *audience*.

We recognize several objectives for the listening congregation.
1. To gain information
2. To experience support from corporate expressions of faith
3. To reach judgments
   a. About the message preached
   b. About faith concerns and issues
   c. About future action
4. To receive renewal
   a. To be stimulated
   b. To be confirmed in attitudes
   c. To be revivified in faith
5. To respond to the varied stimuli present in the service of worship.

Objectives such as these may be attained by the good listeners who attend the service of worship. Such hearers (1) give attention readily, (2) sustain interest throughout the service, particularly within the elements of the service where the participation requested is active listening, (3) reinforce the speaker principally through nonverbal signals during the preaching of the message, and (4) respond through decision or through appreciative and informed comment at the close of the service.

Research into listening behavior[4] reveals characteristics which effect the level of capability which individuals may bring to the hearing of the gospel:

*Personal Factors*
1. Intelligence and facility with language
   a. Reading comprehension
   b. Recognition of correct English usage
   c. Size of vocabulary
2. Ability to make inferences
   a. Discern relationships among ideas
   b. Differentiate between main and subsidiary concepts
3. Experience in listening to difficult material
4. Use of special techniques to improve concentration
   a. Structurize the message
   b. Mental review
   c. Note-taking
5. Absence or presence of fatigue

*Subject Factors*
1. Real interest in the subject
2. Emotional adjustment to the subject
3. Ability to see significance in the subject

*Speaker Factors*
1. Speaker effectiveness
2. Audibility of speaker
3. Energy expenditure of the speaker
4. Admiration of speaker
5. Emotional adjustment to the speaker

*Setting Factors*
1. Temperature of room
2. Ventilation of room

## The Social Basis of Preaching

3. Presence of distractions
4. Number of persons present in relation to room size

That listening is a learned behavior suggests that the educational ministry of the church could aid the congregation in the development of listening skills. Certainly the ministers will wish to minimize the negative impact of the speaker, subject, and setting factors cited above.

Listening may be facilitated by strategies similar to the following:

1. Establish expectation of listening effectiveness as characteristic of the congregation.
2. Provide good models for listening by those in the congregation's direct line of vision: the ministers and the choir.
3. Encourage adults to model good listening for young worshipers.
4. Be responsive to feedback (in the form of post-service comment). Encourage direct comment on the message.
5. Offer praise for evidence of good listening.
6. Afford younger listeners listening targets by suggesting in church school that they listen for particular information in the message.
7. Facilitate note-taking on the reverse side of the worship folder.
8. Recognize the relative shortness of attention spans.
9. Alter movement patterns: Do not keep the congregation in one posture too long.

*What do you know about the congregation?* An audience may be described by the degree of cohesiveness characteristic of those who compose it, the level of

homogeneity present, the commonality of purpose and participation evidenced by the group, and their perception of worthwhile goals to which their presence contributes. Audiences range from the spontaneous groups to the disciplined audience. The former possesses few of the factors which identify well-organized groups; the latter possesses high degrees of all the factors conditioned by prior training, complete orientation, indoctrination, and regimentation.[5] A congregation is a selected audience characterized by
1. A common basis for membership
2. Accepted group objectives
3. Common ground
4. Homogeneous character reflected in similar values, attitudes, and expectations.

A congregation new to a preacher should be analyzed as he anticipates preaching to it. Statistical information should be readily available in reports and minutes of groups to which the congregation belongs, associations, conventions, or other bodies. If the minister has been contacted by a committee (pastoral search committee or personnel committee), its composition may be representative of the larger body. Direct questions to the members of the committee may be useful. Indirect assessment of attitudes may be perceived through lines of questions or discussions introduced by its members. General information may be found in
1. Public-opinion polls
2. Federal-state census reports
3. Analysis of election returns (support of candidates and issues)
4. Local newspapers

5. Church bulletins and papers
6. Opinion leaders in the community and in the church

Specific analysis of the congregation will focus upon the extent of group homogeneity, listener knowledge about you, about your subject, and attitudes and opinions about your position/point of view. Group homogeneity will suggest how your listeners cluster and how their opinions are shaped. Among the clues you will examine are:

1. Sex
2. Age
3. Place of residence/social status
4. Education
5. Income level/occupation
6. Race
7. Political preference
8. Religious perspective

This list suggests areas of information about the congregation which may help the preacher anticipate probable response to his message. Characteristics discovered will not shape content except in organization and expression. The preacher must understand the dominant religious perspectives of the congregation if he is to effect change, inspire action, or stimulate existing attitudes. Attitudes regarding contemporary social issues may be discerned through understanding political preferences. The dynamics of group response may be anticipated more accurately when the homogeneity of the congregation is assessed through consideration of each of these factors.

*What do your listeners know about you?* Generally the

congregation's direct knowledge of the minister will be less extensive today than in previous generations. Occasionally, accurate knowledge will be preferable to the idealized image of the minister some in the congregation may fabricate. How the preacher is perceived is an important determinant of the acceptability of his messages, particularly those which deal with realities that may be unpopular or those deemed controversial.

*Ethos* is the hearer's perception of the peacher's character, intelligence, and goodwill.[6] The congregation expects the minister to evidence high moral *character* in all his dealings. While no one expects sinless perfection from the preacher, all acknowledge the leadership of the minister in matters of morality. His judgment is respected in matters of public morality—the difficult issues that confront society. In his personal concerns, the minister is seen as an example in speech, in relationships, in business dealings, and in other areas of individual moral judgment. The minister who commends righteousness and justice to his congregation must himself live out those attributes.

The preacher must be perceived as a person of *intelligence* by his hearers. He will have appropriate training for his calling. His reading and study must represent a major commitment in keeping with the pressures of weekly sermon preparation. His ideas must not only possess freshness and appeal but also must be carefully framed and valid. While the minister will no longer be either the only well-educated or among the few well-educated persons in the community, he nevertheless must merit confidence for his understand-

## The Social Basis of Preaching

ings for they are pivotal and life-shaping. The minister cannot boast of his learning, nor should he pride himself in any area of ignorance from a false sense of humility. The call of God sets the minister upon the high road of knowledge informed by the very truth of God revealed in Christ Jesus, the Lord, illumined through the action of the Holy Spirit who calls to remembrance the deep things of God. "Such knowledge is too wonderful for me; . . . I cannot attain it" (Ps. 139:6) sets a high standard for the person committed to life-transforming knowing through faith. Antiintellectualism is as alien to the faith as is the claim to special, inaccessible knowledge revealed to a select one, upon which no questions or verification are permitted. Both are prideful; both are sin.

Is there a bond of rapport between preacher and people? Do the hearers sense *goodwill* in the attitude of the minister? The recognition that the minister desires only good for his hearers is an essential part of how he is perceived. The minister contributes to that perception of his attitude toward the people he serves not only in what he says but in how he lives a genuine concern for the well-being of his flock. Pretense will be detected at once and may be among the most serious, potentially undermining aspects of his work. While the congregation will extend to the minister the benefit of a doubt, he must validate their confidence continually.

The ethical proof of a minister who is unknown to a congregation may be enhanced through an introduction by a presiding layperson or other worship leader. References to the minister's education, family, experience, and service help the hearers make inferences about his character, intelligence, and goodwill. A false sense of modesty may diminish the response of the hearer if the minister feigns an "aw, shucks" attitude by which he refuses to allow the person introducing him to assist him at the point of sketching his background for the benefit of the hearers and their perception of his *ethos*.

Generally that perception will be advanced by the preacher through references in introductory comments to his pleasure in being with the congregation; his awareness of their history and contributions in ministry; his common ties with them, if any; his background; education; experience; and such personal information as may foster acceptance from the outset of his ministry among them. Two cautions must be stated:

1. The person who introduces the minister must not promise more than can be reasonably delivered.
2. The minister must not be perceived as "tooting his own horn" or as condescending or overly ingratiating in his comments about himself. Humor directed to himself may be an acceptable means of demonstrating his common humanity with his hearers but must, of course, be controlled, relevant, and in good taste.

*What do your listeners know about your subject?* The preacher deals with topics which are well-known to the members of the congregation. The great themes of the faith will figure again and again in the preaching of the church year even though the texts will be many and varied and the titles printed in the worship folders Sunday after Sunday will all be different. Worship calls us to focus upon the elements which speak *anew* the Word of grace. We tell the old, old story of Jesus and His

## The Social Basis of Preaching

love, but that story is spoken anew in each worship encounter.

When the experiences of the congregation are both educational through Bible study and worshipful through the corporate services of the church, similarity of content and theme is inevitable. However, that similarity may not be recognized by all or by most who participate in both. Again, the varied texts from Scriptures which may support consideration of a single theme may infer more variety than is present. Diversity of age, education, vocation, and maturity in faith supports wide divergence in knowledge of the subjects we develop in our sermons.

A well-prepared sermon will offer new insights to all hearers. If the preacher has been claimed by the text, and if he through extensive preparation claims the text for the needs of his hearers, doubtless the Word proclaimed will speak anew to the congregation. Even where the text is well known and the theme is inevitably developed repeatedly, there will be the freshness and appeal of new or rekindled knowledge to edify the listeners. When the sermon cannot be characterized as well prepared, when the preacher has not paid the price for freshness and appeal as he speaks anew the Word of grace, the sermon will not possess the edge it could have. The preacher recognizes its lack; the congregation senses both the preacher's frustration and their sense of disappointment. The sermon ought to stretch the congregation to deeper insight, higher knowledge, and greater commitment. To ask what prior knowledge the hearer shall bring to the message is a vital question the preacher must examine as he prepares to preach. The question after the sermon is similar, What new awareness can the congregation take from this message as a specific result of the preparation and presentation I have invested in the proclamation of this Word from God? Again, How have I built from the known to the unknown to advance knowing? To answer, the preacher must carefully, before he preaches, appraise his hearers' understanding of his subject.

*How do members of the congregation position themselves with respect to the purpose of the sermon?* The congregation is a selected audience most of whom are already believers sympathetic to the preacher and his message. While evangelistic purposes, for example, directed toward conviction and persuasion evolve directly from the nature of New Testament faith, most of the hearers in a typical congregation have already positioned themselves with respect to that intent. To emphasize an evangelistic appeal when there are few if any persons present who can respond will frustrate preacher and people alike.[7] To seek to revitalize faith among persons who have little or no personal commitment would be equally inappropriate.

There is no adequate substitute for the pastor's knowing his people and meditating on their needs as he sets his purpose for the message he prepares. Even when emphases are selected from tradition or calendar, their character must be designed for the people who will hear the message or series of messages. Rural churches, for example, may follow the tradition of one or two revival meetings each year. Tradition dictates a fall series of services with an evangelistic purpose even

## The Social Basis of Preaching

though knowledge of the congregation might suggest instead the need for a revival of intercessory prayer and cultivating a climate of caring in the fellowship.

Occasionally the preacher may find himself addressing an issue which has dramatically polarized the congregation. If he is to become an agent of reconciliation to restore peace, his purpose needs to be evaluated carefully with respect to the attitudes of the congregation. To unknowingly alienate his hearers by failing to consider their attitudes may deny him any role as reconciler. While such attitudes should not dictate the preacher's comprehension of truth or right in the issues, they must not be ignored in his selecting strategies and approaches to effect reconciliation.

Controversy causes individuals to position themselves as favorable, hostile, and neutral or undecided with regard to an issue or action. An approach which makes undecided individuals favorable, hostile individuals undecided or favorable, and confirms those favorable in their viewpoint would be deemed successful. While in deliberative bodies a simple majority, 51 percent would constitute victory, a church must seek earnestly for a larger percentage of agreement if genuine resolution of differences is to occur.

### The Nature of Congregational Response

The corporate nature of the worship context for proclamation lends support for group or congregational response to the Word spoken. We have stated the view that reciprocal reinforcement, believer to believer, worshiper to worshiper, provides support for the sermon and encourages response. The hearer responds with verbal signals, the appropriate "amen," and nonverbal signals, nodding in agreement or communicating recognition by alertness and involvement in the word spoken.

The order of service which guides the worshipers through the elements of the service includes actions in which all participate: singing, reading, responding, and praying. Such actions anticipate the continuing corporate response to proclamation—listening and decision.

While there are reasonable expectations for such group responsiveness to proclamation, individual response is generally regarded as the primary indicator of effectiveness. The claims of the gospel are, after all, individual in nature. Decision which is life-changing in nature is inevitably made by the life changed. For this reason our appeals are directed toward individuals who, nevertheless, are part of a larger body of individuals who influence one another in decisions reached in the corporate worship setting.

What in our presentation of ideas, our structure of argument, touches the springs of response in our hearers? Why do listeners respond favorably to the sermons we preach? One principal factor is *ethical proof*. We accept ideas and argument as valid from those individuals we trust, respect, and appreciate.

Ideas that answer deep needs and motives we readily accept as possessing strong *ethical appeal*. When our acceptance of the validity of a concept resides in the answering of a deep need or motive operative in our lives, we are being convinced by *emotional proof*. Such support depends for its validity upon the hearer's perception that acceptance of argument contributes to the meeting of one's needs or desires.

We call these areas of response to arguments—the hearer's conviction that they meet needs or desires important to him or her—*motivational appeals.* Listener response is conditioned upon identifiable motives present among all to varying degrees. The so-called higher motives may not be normative until basic motives (needs and desires) are met. When the motives essential to well-being are answered, the listener may respond to the challenge offered by appeal to those we identify as higher.

Thus, the listener listens more willingly, believes arguments more readily, does things advocated by the preacher more promptly when the sermon touches in him a recognized need or desire. These motivational appeals are variously described.[8] Our list moves from the basic life needs to the desirable aspects of living which must await satisfaction of the primary needs. With each we shall illustrate its use by the apostle Paul in his Letter to the Romans.

**Safety and Security**

The basic desire is for survival. If an argument or a recommended action contributes to the probability of essential well-being, we respond favorably to it. We do not court physical danger; we desire that our needs be met presently and into our maturity. We desire happiness in this world and beyond. Until the basic requirements of food, clothing, shelter, safety, and security are met, we cannot easily respond to other appeals.

For he [God] will render to every man according to his works: to those who by patience in well-doing seek for glory and honor and immortality, he will give eternal life; but for those who are factious and do not obey the truth, but obey wickedness, there will be wrath and fury. There will be tribulation and distress for every human being who does evil . . . but glory and honor and peace for every one who does good (Rom. 2:6-11).

## Social Acceptance and Approval

We may observe a microcosm of humanity in the emerging consciousness of an infant. Initially the baby seeks only to have her personal needs met: food and comfort. Gradually she perceives that persons meet those needs. She assumes that to be their primary function. But she discovers that they seem motivated by an emotion unnamed even as they are unnamed. By the time she recognizes the essential nature of their care, she discovers the magic results of a smile beneficently bestowed upon them. Their response sets up a pattern which will last a lifetime: She experiences acceptance and approval. If the argument demonstrates that action or ideas accepted will endow us with the good opinion of others, if we will be accepted, appreciated, recognized by those we value, we shall accept that argument.

"For the kingdom of God is not food and drink but righteousness and peace and joy in the Holy Spirit; he who thus serves Christ is acceptable to God and approved by men" (Rom. 14:17-18).

## Acquisitiveness

Possessions are important to us. When they become the leading motivational principle of our living so that we pull down our barns to build greater barns, go away from Christ sorrowful for we have great possessions, or when we assume that life does consist in the abundance of possessions, then the good in this need or desire is lost. To say that the motive can be distorted is not to deny its legitimate function in provident care for our needs and for those who depend upon us. A prerequisite to stewardship is possessions entrusted to be employed faithfully. Scriptures emphasize the character of eternal treasure or worth and appeal to our genuine desire to obtain the pearl of great price, living water, inexhaustible life.

When you were slaves of sin, you were free in regard to righteousness. But then what return did you get from the things of which you are now ashamed? The end of those things is death. But now that you have been set free from sin and have become slaves of God, the return you get is sanctification and its end, eternal life. For the wages of sin is death, but the free gift of God is eternal life in Christ Jesus our Lord (Rom. 6:20-23).

**Adventure**

The call to excitement is strong. The unknown beckons us. We are eager to explore, to experience the unusual, the new. Abraham is a hero among the faithful because he left Ur of the Chaldees with neither map nor compass. He responded to the command to go "to the land that I will show you" (Gen. 12:1). The romance of missions at home and, particularly, abroad we perceive as a call to high adventure with God. When the life of faith is seen as an adventure, something exciting, out of the ordinary, we shall find ready response to our invitation.

"O the depth of the riches and wisdom and knowledge of God! How unsearchable are his judgments and how inscrutable his ways!" (Rom. 11:33).

## Freedom

Everyone desires to be free from external restraint. The individual rightly judges that realization of potential is contingent upon appropriate freedom. We contrast freedom exercised responsibly with license, the perversion of a good by selfishness, by self-gratification which often infringes upon the freedom of others. The paradox of freedom only through submission, acknowledging the lordship of Christ, places the emphasis correctly for the Christian. It is an often-encountered motif in the New Testament.

"Because the creation itelf will be set free from its bondage to decay and obtain the glorious liberty of the children of God" (Rom. 8:21).

## Response to Beauty

The creature gained from the Creator the capacity to recognize beauty and to appreciate creation: the sea pounding upon the craggy shoreline; the giant redwoods ascending, ascending; the delicate pattern of white against green in Queen Anne's lace; the majesty of the Brahms requiem; the Michelangelo Sistine Chapel ceiling alike evoke an appreciation and pleasurable response.

> Ever since the creation of the world his invisible nature, namely, his eternal power and deity, has been clearly perceived in the things that have been made. So they are

without excuse; for although they knew God they did not honor him as God or give thanks to him, but they became futile in their thinking and their senseless minds were darkened. Claiming to be wise they became fools, and exchanged the glory of the immortal God for images resembling mortal man or birds or animals or reptiles (Rom. 1:20-23).

### Altruism

We seek the welfare of others. This motive brings us full circle: from personal security as determinant of response to caring for and wishing to assure the welfare of others. Great saints of all ages have lived in response to this motive for service. Certainly his desire for the welfare of his brethren evoked from the apostle Paul the ringing hyperbole,

"For I could wish that I myself were accursed and cut off from Christ for the sake of my brethren, my kinsmen by race" (Rom. 9:3).

### Conclusion

The employment of movitational appeals acknowledges that harnessing our needs and desires to the service of sound argument is appropriate. Like proof which resides in the preacher, proof which flows from appeals to hearer's needs and desires must be combined with rational, logical proof which resides in the material of the argument itself. If the evidence and support for our ideas are compelling, their acceptance becomes likely when their presentation the preacher combines with *ethos* and *pathos:* ethical and emotional proof. We defer our discussion of logical proof until we consider the topic of support for the message: the logical basis of preaching.

There are three principles regarding the operation of motivational appeals that must be kept in mind by the preacher:
1. Values based upon needs and desires do not occur in isolation but in interaction one with another.
2. Psychologists have identified hierarchies of values which identify physiological needs as basic and higher motives as possible only after basic needs are met.
3. Such hierarchies of values vary according to cultural constraints.

### A Reciprocal Integrity—Pastor and People

We will never fully realize the communicative thrust of preaching without the operation of reciprocal integrity as a part of the social dimension of proclamation. Integrity is possible when pastor and people agree that the center of worship and preaching is the eternal God revealed in Christ Jesus, the Lord. His truth, justice, and righteousness set the theme of our service to Him. These qualities must permeate the preaching and hearing of the gospel.

The sermon benefits from support which stems from the commonality in faith which affects the reception of the Word spoken. Such support, however, must not be taken for granted. While we may assume its operation, that common faith facilitates the speaking and hearing of the gospel, we must not presume upon that fact. To assess the health of faith held in common by pastor and people, we recommend an ongoing, three-stage process.

## The Social Basis of Preaching

### Faith Expressed in Dialogue

The proclamation of the Word must not answer questions no one is asking. If the program of preaching seems to be predicated upon the assumption that communication is one-way only, pastor to people, the development of common faith will be hampered. Dialogue occurs in a limited way during the presentation of the message as nonverbal response follows verbal and nonverbal signals. The pastor must be sensitive to needs of his congregation as he prepares and presents his messages. Dialogue can clarify needs and appraise the degree such needs are met in preaching. Lay expression of faith encourages thought and precision of belief and its statement. One church introduced an element in its service of worship called "Word from the World," a lay testimony focusing upon the faith component supporting varied vocations. Such statements juxtaposed with the sermon facilitated dialogue as a feature of worship.

### Faith Clarified in Dialectic

Dialectic is logical argument directed toward the discovery of the truth of a theory or opinion. The classical model presupposes two knowledgeable individuals moving together through a series of probing questions to a conclusion. One of the parties possesses a more secure hold on truth. The other seeks wisdom comparable to his colleague's but approaches such attainment cautiously. The conversation between Nicodemus and Jesus in John 3 suggests the procedure of dialectic. Indeed, the apologetic nature of the postconversation comment by John conveys the sense of logical argument based upon supposed questions which would grow out of Jesus's comments.

The preacher should encourage dialectic as a means of clarifying the faith held in common by the members of the congregation. Since faith concerns require the establishment of presuppositions which can't be fully proved with empirical evidence, dialectic is a means of approaching faith we would do well to claim within the body of the church. Faith is a way of knowing that transcends the operation either of logic or scientific (or psuedoscientific) investigation. Faith may precede the acceptance of specific doctrines and authority structures. Once grasped, however, faith must be nurtured and encouraged to mature through our preaching. Dialectic must augment our preaching strategy if we are to make disciples.

### Faith Refined Through Discipleship

Discipleship is the goal of our preaching. We preach Jesus as Lord. Our response to Him molds us into a people whose community receives its highest and best expression when He is acknowledged as Lord.

While we may seek to impose a hierarchy of submission which will somehow give us status in the scheme, the doctrine of the priesthood of the believer and the conviction that ultimate allegiance belongs only to God corroborate the knowledge that every individual Christian has, as a result of faith, communion with God which is life-changing and priority-setting. Only as we accept our role as disciples can we become a people under God, submissive to His will, growing in faith and in witness to a world in need of the Word we share as people of God. Discipleship is less a matter of office than attitude. The attitude is submission to the discipline of the Lord.

## The Preacher's Motivation

The preacher-pastor must move from a stance of personal integrity as he leads his people toward discipleship through dialogue and dialectic. To appraise his ministry the minister must examine his motivation in light of these touchstones:
1. *The ministry must be constructive.* The biblical Word is edifying, building up.
2. *The ministry must be caring.* The model for ministry in the Scriptures is one of compassion. Jesus was "moved with compassion." There is no explanation for the selfless service we encounter in the biblical narrative more descriptive than that which emanates from compassion.
3. *The ministry must be clear.* Our motives must be transparent, open to scrutiny.
4. *The ministry must be conscionable.* We are to be just. Our service must be conformable to conscience.

The minister must not become a manipulator. Indeed, if his service conforms to the standards summarized in the guidelines articulated, he cannot manipulate. Manipulative strategies cannot have transparent motives. The pastor's agenda when he manipulates must be hidden. Occasionally from a superior moral awareness or identification with insight which would be difficult and time consuming to replicate in the consideration of others, the minister may feel justified in manipulation: worthy ends, after all, justify questionable means. This approach inevitably undermines the preacher's integrity and will lead to diminished effectiveness. The temptation to ignore just or right use of motivational appeals in combination with logical and reasoned argument must be resisted. His role as interpreter of Scripture must not be perverted by forcing the text to support his position in the lowest use of proof-texting. He must not lay claim to being the sole recipient of special insight to establish his point. He should carefully weigh the probable results of withholding information, explanation, or insights as over against his personal commitment to speaking the truth in love.

After all, the social basis of our preaching encounters its most profound expression in the context of Christian love. A loving people and a loving minister validate the promise that God is love in a world otherwise devoid of *agape*, selfless, self-giving love. Such a context confirms reciprocal integrity and the responsibility of active speaking and hearing the Word among those who gather for corporate worship.

### Think on These Things

1. How can the minister evaluate the listening behavior of the congregation? Note positive listening characteristics. Negative ones.
2. What are the implications of the following Scriptures for our preaching: Mark 12:37 and John 7:46?
3. What are ways corporate response to preaching may be expressed? Encouraged?
4. Explain the following statement: "Manipulation of the congregation is an unethical approach to achieving response." Can you cite instances where manipu-

lation seemed to be employed as a substitute for more acceptable strategies?
5. Complete word studies upon *listen, hear,* and *integrity.*
6. The gospel is in competition with many contemporary claims upon the minds of persons. What forms does this competition take? How can the minister as spokesperson successfully gain a hearing for the gospel in the face of this competition?
7. What did Jesus mean by, "He who has ears, let him hear" (Matt. 13:9)?
8. Prepare to introduce a colleague to a group. Consciously strive to enhance his or her ethical appeal among the hearers.
9. Find examples in sermons of a minister's use of motivational appeals to gain acceptance of ideas.

**Suggested Readings**

Allen, Ronald and Gordon Borror. *Worship: Rediscovering the Missing Jewel.* Portland, Ore.: Multnomah Press, 1982.

Jensen, J. Vernon. *Perspectives on Oral Communication.* Boston: Holbrook Press, Inc., 1970.

Martin, Ralph P. *The Worship of God.* Grand Rapids: William B. Eerdmans Publishing Company, 1982.

Gray, Giles Wilkeson and Claude Merton Wise. *The Bases of Speech.* 3rd ed. New York: Harper & Row, Publishers, 1959.

Oliver, Robert T., Harold P. Zelko, and Paul D. Holtzman. *Communicative Speaking and Listening,* 4th ed. New York: Holt, Rinehart and Winston, Inc., 1968.

Randolph, David James. *God's Party: A Guide to New Forms of Worship.* Nashville: Abingdon, 1975.

Snyder, Ross. *Contemporary Celebration.* Nashville: Abingdon, 1971.

White, James F. *Introduction to Christian Worship.* Nashville: Abingdon, 1981.

Willimon, William H., *Word, Water, Wine and Bread.* Valley Forge, Pa.: Judson Press, 1980.

### Notes

1. Evelyn Underhill, *Worship* (New York: Harper and Row, 1936), p. 81.

2. Use of a communications model has been a helpful addition to textbooks in interpersonal communication and public speaking for the past two decades. The concept came to our attention through David K. Berlo, *The Process of Communication* (New York: Holt, Rinehart and Winston, 1960).

3. David H. C. Read, *Sent from God* (Nashville, Abingdon Press, 1974), p. 54.

4. Research into listening behavior is an area of study the preacher should examine. Thomas R. Lewis and Ralph G. Nichols, *Speaking and Listening* (Dubuque: William C. Brown Company, 1965) effectively combines research findings and practical suggestions for the speaker.

5. Robert C. Jeffrey and Owen Peterson, *Speech A Text with Adapted Reading*, 2nd ed. (New York: Harper and Row, 1975), pp. 102-103.

6. Ethical proof or appeal has been recognized as important since the Greek writers on rhetoric first articulated its significance. Aristotle's *Rhetoric*, Book II, chapters 12—17, discusses its impact upon audiences.

7. An interesting discussion of the intentions of the preacher revolves about the question, "Which of the four is the one employed most in preaching." The singular significance of the intention, to stimulate, emerges from such consideration.

8. While motive appeals are variously described, we are indebted to the standard work of Giles Wilkeson Gray and Waldo W. Braden, *Public Speaking Principles and Practice*, 2nd ed., (New York: Harper and Row, 1963), p. 151 *ff.*

# 4

## The Logical Basis of Preaching

Our discussion of *proof* operative in the speaker and the hearer in the preceding chapter anticipated in our sermons the action of logical proof—that support which resides in the material of the message. We may be hesitant to speak of *proof* in sermons or, for that matter, of *logic*. Somehow our sermons, we believe, rest upon an authority that makes proof unnecessary and logic, perhaps, impossible.

In another age, possibly; in our time, a sermon without support will enjoy a hesitant hearing at best. The preacher of such a sermon will establish little, convince few, and successfully call to action only those who act without reflection. The failure of our sermons to influence lives for long-term change may be a result of our lack of concern for the telling power of argument crafted from the validity of our text and the consciousness of the power of information included to support the concepts of our sermons.

### The Nature of Inference

Inference may be defined as the process of arriving at a conclusion through the consideration of reasoned argument based upon the presentation of supporting information. Informally we understand inference to be the means by which we change our minds, have our beliefs confirmed, or accept a challenge to action. When the preacher cites the depth of personal commitment of Francis of Assisi, we infer that our lives could be deepened spiritually by a like commitment. When the minister recalls vividly the selfless gift of life through a retelling of the gospel story of Christ's passion, we find our understanding of *agape* rekindled. When the example of Christian zeal in the mission of Adoniram Judson comes alive in the sermon, we accept the challenge to personal witness where we find missionary opportunity afforded us. Inference changes, confirms, or motivates because we see the compelling validity of each of the illustrations included by the preacher.

We arrive at a conclusion as active listeners. If the argument has been carefully crafted by the preacher, if the sermon speaks to us as it spoke to the preacher, we may reach the conclusion to which he has been led in his study of the material. Occasionally our response to the material will differ from that of the preacher because our preceding experiences do not correspond with his. We may be cynical. We may be still in the throes of an emotional loss which the material of the sermon causes us to feel anew. We may go beyond the intention of the preacher, finding in his support a compelling urgency he has neither encountered nor articulated.

The study must reveal to the preacher the desired conclusion and the probable presence of other inferences discernible in his material or in his presentation of the message. Whether the preacher determines to reach

*The Logical Basis of Preaching*

the sermon conclusion from deduction or induction, he must clearly anticipate the desired end of the message.

The hearers consider reasoned argument. Rational faculties must be employed as the sermon is preached. Christians or those who seek faith do not check their reasoning in some anteroom before they enter the sanctuary where the holy words will be heard. The pastor as priest who mediates the message of God to people must approach his task rationally. He must stimulate reasoning. He does this by structuring the presentation so that concepts *follow:* acceptance of this piece of information as valid leads to the confirmation of this position in the sermon. We, as hearers, recognize sound judgment and good sense in the presentation of the ideas of the sermon. We judge that they are valid; that judgment is *reason.*

The hearer accepts the credibility of reasoned argument through an assessment of the quality of the supporting material included in the sermon. We prefer the term *support* to *proof* because we operate in a sphere where proof is inevitably elusive. When we preach, we support our argument often through reference to the Scriptures. We depend upon the power and convicting presence of the Holy Spirit. We know faith in the hearer to be responsive to faith in the preacher. While the convinced believer will see these characteristics of our messages as possessing a compelling credibility, the nonbeliever or the believer whose faith is wavering requires *support* in the form of reasoned argument to accept the validity of the concepts proclaimed in the sermon. Thus, the convincing force of the argument depends upon the hearers' perception of the support for the ideas of the message. The support complements the faith of the believer and brings the nonbeliever to acceptance of the validity of the message. The nonbeliever experiences the confirmation of the message's ultimate credibility and receives the gift of faith through the action of the Holy Spirit.

**The Use of Evidence**

Evidence in a sermon is the material which supports the line of reasoning we present. An argument is persuasive when its acceptance follows a review of the material presented. If the evidence conforms to our understanding of what is likely or probable, we accept the argument as valid. If the evidence demonstrates an insight we have previously determined to be valid, our prior understanding confirms the validity of the argument as now presented. Occasionally the argument simply makes sense. We do not analyze the reason; we merely accept the argument since we believe it follows from the ideas presented in support. We accept the claim or logical link present in the argument.

Let us turn now to a consideration of the specific forms of supporting material useful to explanation and persuasion in sermons. We have previously identified the complementary dimensions of the minister's task in proclamation—teaching and preaching. When our goal is to achieve comprehension, we shall find these forms of support particularly useful: specific details or characteristics, examples, description, narration, definition, comparison, contrast, and statistics. When our goal is to motivate to action, we shall depend upon similar forms of support with particular stress upon specific instances, statistics, comparisons, testimony of authority, and causal argument.

*Specific Details or Characteristics.* Explanation requires the assimilation of specific information, details, or characteristics of an object (the ark of the covenant), an event (the Passover), or a concept (stewardship). The dimensions of the ark, its features, the craftsmanship which it represented, its function as symbol, the mercy seat are details to foster understanding of this object from Old Testament worship. The impetus for the Passover observance, its value as a teaching device, its focus upon the family, its use of prescribed language recalling deliverance, the menu with its symbolic values are significant details to enable our hearers to deepen their awareness of the nature of the supper. Stewardship reflects our total commitment to God, God's ownership of all, our faithfulness, the joy of sharing, the tithe as a biblical standard for giving—details to enhance the understanding of this concept.

*Examples* are specific instances or, in a more detailed expansion of specific instances, illustrations. Again, a condensed illustration is a specific instance. "Elderly women who possessed unusual piety and a willingness to serve were identified as widows in the early church" is a specific instance. *Interpretation* is an example of the gifts of the Spirit. The apostle Paul, to validate his ministry, detailed the miraculous nature of his conversion on the Damascus road to illustrate his genuine experience in faith and its transforming power.[1]

*Descriptions* convey images or impressions chosen to reveal the appearance, nature or attributes of an object. We may describe the woman at the well as one shunned by her neighbors since she went alone at an unlikely time to draw water. Her careworn face mirrored the rejection of others. Her hesitant response to Jesus' request indicated her surprise that He, a man, a Jew, would speak to her. Her playful banter suggested that she had often spoken with men in the easy equality of the casual male-female encounter. She became disquieted when the conversation turned to spiritual matters. Finally she left the well with joy born of amazement, "Come see a man who told me . . ." (John 4:29). The event described takes on a significance which stems from the impact of its nature heightened thereby.

*Narration.* As a form of supporting material, narration supplies details and description to heighten understanding of an action or event. To turn the description of the encounter of Jesus and the woman at the well into a narrative, one simply adds the chronology of the events to form the story. Illustrations will often be narratives in form; indeed a complete sermon may be developed as a narrative to present a biblical truth. Here, however, we focus upon the nature of narrative as supporting material. When we sense the validity, the likelihood, the probability of an event through its narration, the principle of support through narration is operative. New Testament preaching narrated the gospel, the events of Christ's coming, ministry, death, burial, resurrection, appearances, ascension, and expected, imminent return. Preaching in its initial form was the telling and retelling of his story by an eyewitness, a convinced narrator.

*Definitions.* When we define, we use language to foster understanding of a term or concept which otherwise is

obscure or unknown. We provide *meaning*. The preacher must be aware that his hearers speak less and less the specialized theological vocabulary so much a part of the minister's life. What does *grace* mean? The general response, unmerited favor, may be little more than a starting place, but it is that. An approximate synonym is *mercy*. To define the concept, we must first identify the general class and then differentiate through citing particulars the specific nature of that item within the class. Thus, *grace* is a property of God's love akin to mercy; through grace God communicates, reveals his love particularly in the death and resurrection of Jesus, and grants victory to those who respond to his love in faith.[2] Definitions may be most communicative when they have been formed by the preacher himself—informed certainly by careful study and thoughtful deliberation. Approaches to definition include, the following:
1. Definition by synonym
2. Definition by example
3. Definition by details
4. Definition by classification and differentiation
5. Definition by comparison and contrast
6. Definition by historical background
7. Definition by etymology
8. Definition by operation, action, or purpose
9. Definition by negation
10. Combination of methods[3]

*Comparison.* Support by *comparison* details similarities between two like subjects or concepts. Metaphors and similes are figures of speech based upon comparison, the former an implied comparison, the latter a stated comparison which employs "like" or "as." The early church compared itself to Noah's ark, the church in the comparison becoming the ark of salvation. A contemporary example describes faith as trust expressed in action or commitment which we explain through comparison to belief that a chair will support our weight expressed through entrusting our weight to the chair. Jesus taught often with comparison. Matthew 13 records teachings of the kingdom expressed as comparison: "The kingdom of heaven may be compared to a man who sowed good seed in his field" (v. 24*b*).

*Contrast.* Usually associated with comparison, contrast clarifies through citing differences. "Unlike the civic club where membership offers social activities and service opportunities which are more or less optional, the church offers members the challenge of total commitment which dramatically transforms our social values and service orientation. Motives in dynamic church membership are God-ordained and others-directed." That is an example of contrast as support.

*Statistics.* Defined simply as numbers, statistics condense data and provide complicated information through summation in numerical form. To emphasize the shift in our population to older persons as a basis for reorientation of the church's strategy in decades to come, the minister would find statistics useful. "As this century grows older, so does the population. The fastest growing group in the United States today are those over 50. In fact, this year is the first time those over 65 outnumber teenagers. Today, almost 25 percent of adults in school are 45 years or older."[4] Numbers need interpretation and simplification. Note that in the example cited, the raw figures become percentages or totals made more meaningful through comparisons. Citation of numbers without interpretation heads the list of material difficult to listen to, if not downright boring.

*Testimony of Authority.* Inexperienced preachers may feel that the inclusion of statements or interpretations of others within a sermon will weaken the impact of the message if these are credited to those responsible for them. There is, of course, an ethical demand that credit be given where credit is due. But citation of sources, indications that noted individuals in the fields of biblical scholarship or interpretation support your point, strengthens the hearers' grasp of the significance of your sermon and their identification of your study with that of other respected authorities.

Citing George Buttrick on prayer or Thomas Merton on the contemplative life will strengthen your point if your hearers appreciate the contributions of these two men in our century. To say, "George Buttrick, whose benchmark work on prayer continues to mold our apprehension of this significant aspect of Christian faith, cites the pivotal necessity of the acceptance of forgiveness after we ask for and receive it,"[5] supplies the essential information to assure response to the insight quoted.

*Causal Argument.* Employing causal argument recognizes a relationship which may be stated: this, therefore this. From statistics regarding population trends toward more persons sixty-five and older than teenagers, the argument may be presented that the church should reorder its programming, planning, and facilities development toward the needs of senior adults. The relationship is cause-effect. Argument based upon cause to effect requires the presentation of support and its interpretation: "Because of this, it follows that . . ." is the statement of the case when causal reasoning is present.

How do we test evidence or support for argument we include in our sermons? There are some helpful principles that should be kept in mind.

1. Does the supporting material do what I intend by its inclusion in my message? If I spend as much time explaining the meaning of the material I include as I do stating it, I probably should reconsider its use.
2. Is the supporting material clear? In the form I intend to use it, will it be immediately intelligible to my hearers? Does its significance depend upon prior understandings my hearers are likely to possess or that I can briefly supply?
3. Can the hearer verify the supporting material from his or her experience or are its exceptional characteristics noted and explained?
4. Am I able to state the supporting material so that its authenticity is clear to the hearer? Must I be indefinite because I lack precise information? "Somewhere I read recently" begins weakly. "A recent Gallup poll revealed . . . ," is little better. "All of us recognize . . . ," should, then, remain unsaid.
5. Where historical perspectives are required, do I possess them for understanding and stating their relevance to others? Do my comparisons, contrasts, descriptions, or narrations suffer because my

antecedent study of historical or biblical contexts was superficial or hurried? Are there notable exceptions of which I am unaware?
6. Can my use of objective data be described as accurate and compelling? Are statistics gathered properly and interpreted accurately? Do the numbers support what I imply? Have I included only those numbers which support my case?
7. When I quote from authority, is my source known to my hearers? respected by them? qualified *in the area* upon which I shall quote him? unbiased?
8. Is my information recent? Biblical scholarship has advanced in the past three decades. When we cite scholars active in the nineteenth century, are we being honest with our hearers unless we corroborate the information with more recent understandings?

Support within a message has cumulative effect. An overall assessment of your use of support probably states, The message was well prepared. It obviously is the result of careful study and preparation. More subtle is the response of agreement or decision to act on the basis of the force of argument. Test the cumulative power of your argument to ascertain its compelling strength. Too much support may diminish the effect of your case because it seems dogmatic to the point of eliminating contrary positions. The preacher builds the best case he can for his position. He cannot have the final word on all subjects however. To suggest that he does through argumentative overkill may seriously undermine his effectiveness with thoughtful hearers.

Whether the preacher develops his message deduc-

# Chart 3
## Models for Argument

*Deductive Model*

**Beginning**

Affirmation of the sermon derived from the text, stated as a general principle

Affirmation, for

**Middle**

Application of the general principle to areas of corporate and personal need in specific aspect one, based upon
    Supporting material: definition, and
    Supporting material: example, and
    Supporting material: narration.

etc.

Specific aspect one, for
    $SM^1$, and
    $SM^2$, and
    $SM^3$.
and
Specific aspect two, for
    $SM^1$, and
    $SM^2$, and
    $SM^3$.
and
Specific aspect three, for
    $SM^1$, and
    $SM^2$.

**End**

Affirmation demonstrably valid as applied in specific aspects of the message

Since $SA^1$, $SA^2$, and $SA^3$, Then affirmation

Accept the affirmation

Appeal

# The Logical Basis of Preaching

## Inductive Model

**Beginning**

Identification of corporate and/or personal need addressed through the text — Need identification

**Middle**

Through the examination of
    Supporting material: definition, and
    Supporting material: example, and
    Supporting material: narration
Specific aspect 1 of the affirmation emerges
Etc.

Through
    $SM^1$, and
    $SM^2$, and
    $SM^3$, emerges
specific aspect 1.
Through
    $SM^1$, etc., emerges
specific aspect 2.
Through
    $SM^1$, etc., emerges
specific aspect 3.

**End**

Examination of the specific aspects to form a general principle, affirmation, demonstrably valid for meeting personal and corporate need.

$SA^1$, $SA^2$, and $SA^3$ form affirmation.

Accept and apply the affirmation — Appeal

tively or inductively, he presents supporting material related to progressive movement perceived as separate aspects or divisions of the sermon. The clichéd three points and a poem has fallen from favor principally because it represents deductive development in a static stereotype uncomfortably close to reality. We have only partially developed a form to put in place of the cliché. But we know it must be dynamic, related to the text perceived through hermeneutical advances, and relevant to contemporary thought and human needs, personal and corporate. A model for contemporary preaching must capture these characteristics.

In the foregoing models based upon deductive and inductive reasoning, statement of affirmation varies. Deductive preaching announces the affirmation from the outset of the message. Inductive preaching leads the hearer to comprehension of the affirmation within or upon the conclusion of the message. Again, use of supporting material differs one from the other. In deductive preaching the unit of argument[6] may be diagramed as follows:

$SA^1$, for

$SM^1$, since a valid causal relationship may be demonstrated between $SM^1$ and $SA^1$;

and

$SM^2$, since a valid causal relationship may be demonstrated between $SM^2$ and $SA^1$.

The important terms are the conjunctions *for* and *since*. The SA is valid for (because of) SM since a causal relationship between the two may be demonstrated.

In inductive preaching, the unit of argument changes, as follows:

# The Logical Basis of Preaching

Through SM¹
Emerges SA¹, since a reasonable connection between SM¹ and SA¹ may be demonstrated.
Through SM²
Emerges SA¹, since a reasonble connection between SM² and SA¹ may be demonstrated

The differentiating terms are the conjunctions *through* and *since* and the distinctive pattern of arrangement coupled with the use of the verb, *emerges*. The diagram enables us to sense the cumulative force of support. When the point is established, there is sufficient force to the argument.

## Faith as Support

Preaching parts company with other forms of public address when we acknowledge the effect of faith corporately manifested between minister and congregation. We have already observed that the congregation is a selected audience since it has among other characteristics a common basis for membership, common ground, and homogeneous character. To an extent, each of these characteristics is predicated upon faith. While there will be among those gathered to hear us preach in our churches some who have not yet presented themselves for membership upon confession or statement of faith, by far the largest percentage present has acknowledged this basis for fellowship within the corporate body.

What does this mean to the preacher? It means, first, that there is an openness to the message unlikely to be present in a spontaneous group or a randomly gathered body of hearers. Second, faith speaks to faith more convincingly than faith to unfaith, given identical structure and support of argument. Third, faith extends to faith the benefit of the doubt: When the evidence is partial, the argument may be accepted on the basis of the prior agreement present among preacher and hearers. Fourth, the experience of faith in the hearer facilitates the apprehension of concepts or actions which are faith based. Fifth, traditions and writings related to faith encounter acceptance of arguments based upon them by those who appreciate their validity because of faith. Sixth, the person of faith gathers for corporate worship in part to experience confirmation and reaffirmation of faith: This expectation fosters acceptance of concepts which tend to confirm and reaffirm. Seventh, faith operative in hearing horizontally affects the response of those others present who also hear in faith.

Since commonality of faith so profoundly affects hearer response, the preacher may be tempted to speak only in pious generalizations guaranteed to evoke predictable praise. He may sense the congregation's willingness to accept proclamation of easily recognized clichés. They may respond favorably to such messages, but there will be limited growth discernible in the lives of those in the fellowship or, indeed, in the fellowship itself, measured in terms of either active involvement or in size of membership. Commonality of faith must be foundational for growth to greater maturity in faith. It must be an invaluable tool for stirring and stretching the hearers to deeper perception and more active personal response in faith than would be possible without preaching.

Again, the preacher must not ignore those among his

*The Logical Basis of Preaching*

hearers who do not yet possess the unifying characteristic of faith. In his reaching out to these hearers through reasoned, supported arguments, the preacher will stir memory of commitment already present among the hearers who attend with faith. Stimulation of a renewed awareness of commitment made in the past reinforces present faith responsiveness.

Faith and reason are both ways of perceiving reality. Since faith is a noun, it is difficult to cast into a sentence in the manner we can employ reason, both a noun and a verb. When we reason together, we corporately approach reality. We weigh evidence; we assess the validity of causal relationships; and we rationally move from an old perspective to a new one. Faith in the Old Testament specified in the high confession of Deuteronomy 6:4, the Shema, "Hear, O Israel: The Lord our God is one Lord" finds verbal expression in *hear*. Faith is *to hear the Word of the Lord*. In the New Testament, the verb is *believe*. Romans 10:9 presents this concept: "If you confess with your lips that Jesus is Lord and *believe in your heart* that God has raised him from the dead, you will be saved" (authors' italics).

Faith as hearing the word of God and as believing in your heart, the place where you know profoundly, is action which enables the individual to perceive reality at its deepest level: Truth, God. Faith affords an approach to knowing complementary to reason and superior to it. And yet, people do not renounce reason when they come to faith. They find reason enriched by new, profound knowledge revealed in the Word of God, the *Logos* of John 1, confirmed by the action of the Holy Spirit who guides into all the truth (John 16:13).

## The Bible as Authority

The role of the Scriptures in supporting the ideas of sermons often is assumed. We take for granted the presence of Scriptures as the beginning place for sermon preparation. Careful and complete study and interpretation of the text we deem imperative as the message comes into being in the study. The minister seeks corroboration of his understandings through reference to other passages of Scripture outside the lesson or text of the message. Generally, frequent references to this further scriptural support will be made during the preaching of the sermon.

How are we to understand the use of Scripture as support? We have already noted the impact of faith in the acceptance of the church's traditions and writings. Significant among the writings which have developed within the body of Christian believers is, of course, the Bible. A confessed believer honors the Scriptures and accepts their witness to the truth revealed in Christ. His or her acceptance of the distinctive nature of the literature of faith which makes up the canon of Holy Scriptures grants probitive force to arguments, affirmations, and specific aspects we include within our messages.

The Christian hearer accepts the Bible as appropriate and strong support within the sermon because of the church's teaching, based upon the Scriptures' record of its authenticity and the historical dependence of the church upon the revealed and written Word, that it is "inspired by God" (2 Tim. 3:16). When the inspired Word is text, the believer listens to the message based

## The Logical Basis of Preaching

upon it. When the preacher uses the Scriptures to witness to the validity of the specific aspects of the sermon, the believer accepts the support the Scriptures afford and the concept articulated.

Readiness to accept the Scriptures as support may create potentially harmful situations. On the one hand, the hearer may be undiscriminating in his or her hearing and accepting concepts offered with biblical support. The unscrupulous use of proof-texting may lead a hearer to accept a nonbiblical idea advanced with presumed biblical support. On the other hand, the nonbeliever may feel that he or she must reject arguments based solely upon Scripture. Dominant or sole use of the Scriptures as support could reduce the probability of favorable response to the message for listeners whose response in faith has yet to be kindled.

Two principles emerge:
1. Recognize the strong support *among believers* for argument from Holy Scriptures; employ that support wisely and well, and the Holy Spirit will honor its use.
2. Couple biblical and extrabiblical support for the components of the messages you preach. The convincing power of the Scriptures will emerge alongside response to concepts that do not require a hearing from faith for acceptance. Again, the Holy Spirit will honor the words spoken to guide the hearers to the Word. "The Bible says" strikes a responsive note only after faith has been discovered through God's grace. Until such time, the minister must speak words which will enable the Word to be heard: His words will be diverse and

calculated to win a responsive hearing from nonbelievers, as well as believers.

## The Objectives of Our Preaching

Logical development of our sermons advances the objectives we seek to attain. These objectives are four in number:
1. To inform
2. To stimulate
3. To convince
4. To persuade

Every sermon we preach will focus primarily upon one of these objectives. As we have stated often, biblical exposition is the genius of all preaching. Exposition is informational. Interpretation is dependent upon information derived from critical areas of investigation. When we preach, it is a rare sermon that does not challenge with new concepts, new teaching. To an extent, then, our preaching is almost always instructive and may be said to have the objective of informing. But the primary objective may be, instead, a purpose other than informing. The preacher must know and state (a task required for knowing) the primary objective the message will attain.

*To inform.* This objective is present to one degree or another in all preaching. It may be dominant in a didactic sermon when the intention is to present in the sermon a basic teaching of Scripture.

*To stimulate.* We seek often to rekindle or revitalize concepts already present (accepted) in the believer. Commitment to these principles has been expressed but needs to be enlivened. A message to revive principles of stewardship or the necessity of witness would have this objective.

*To convince.* The sermon designed to foster agreement with concepts or ideas has the objective to convince. A message on doctrine could have this objective particularly when the issue considered is in the context of a new members' class or when the minister seeks to resolve conflict within a group divided on a doctrinal issue.

*To persuade.* When our aim is action motivated by our message, the objective is to persuade. Generally, persuasion follows conviction: The acceptance of concepts precedes the response in action. When our message is evangelistic, our objective is to persuade. We convince of the need for salvation and offer an invitation to accept forgiveness, acceptance, the response in faith being the action we seek.

The objective of a message will be formulated after a careful study of the text to determine what the scriptural basis of the message is designed to achieve. Again, a grasp of hearer needs will effect our selection of an objective. The nature of the topic upon which we preach will also have a bearing upon our choice of a particular dominant objective for the sermon.

We must be aware, however, that our objectives are not simple or discretely structured. Our aims in a sermon are various and overlapping. They interact with the purposes of our hearers. Some conclusions may be drawn regarding the presence and employment of objectives in our preaching.

1. There is always an objective or objectives which govern any act of preaching/listening.

2. The objective is not always fully recognized by the one preaching or the one listening.
3. Improved communication occurs when the objectives of the preacher and the hearer are similar or may be readily reconciled to one another.
4. Greater familiarity with the objective of the sermon well in advance of preaching the message will enhance its preparation and presentation.

When the objective has been determined, the preacher must relate that objective to the topic of the sermon and the group of hearers anticipated, forming the sermon purpose: My purpose is to convince my hearers that New Testament teaching supports a dynamic but separate relationship between church and state.

The sermon purpose should be framed according to the following criteria:
1. Specificity
2. Achievability
3. Ethical soundness
4. Consistent with the preacher's conduct, acts, and beliefs
5. Of value to the hearers of the message
6. Significant to the preacher
7. Framed to meet spiritual needs

The logical soundness of the message is contingent upon clear purpose statement and awareness of the congregation's expectation—their purpose in listening. While the dominant congregational purpose is often conditioned by prior response to the gospel, the preacher must acknowledge the presence within the congregation of those whose purposes in listening may be to find answers others have already found or to

*The Logical Basis of Preaching*

experience comfort while others receive information or stimulation. Such is the nature of the gospel that it answers needs expressed in many purposes of listeners assembled for worship. The preacher must, of course, possess a sensitivity to the presence of needs and purposes he may address as he preaches from a purpose dominant to his preparation and presentation.

### The Sermon Plan

We recommend that the preacher complete the following sermon plan during the development of his messages:
1. Sermon title
2. Sermon subject
3. Text to be read
4. Other scriptural support
5. Affirmation
6. Objective
7. Sermon purpose

### Think on These Things

1. Examine the concepts *ethos*, *pathos*, and *logos* in standard works on rhetoric or public speaking. Discuss their relevance to preaching.
2. Read five sermons to discover the specific intent of the preachers (to inform, to stimulate, to convince, or to persuade). Find instances in each message where other intentions seem dominant. Copy the excerpt and identify the intention.
3. Formulate your personal definition of faith.
4. Analyze a contemporary sermon with regard to the preacher's use of proof and evidence.

5. Using the model for inductive argument in this chapter, construct an inductive unit of proof for a sermon to convince.
6. Contrast the preacher's use of the Bible as a devotional and a homiletical tool.
7. Outline a procedure for Christian decision making. Does your procedure have implications for problem-solution sermons?
8. What, if any, limitations should we impose upon the use of extrabiblical sources for proof in sermons?
9. Compare Matthew 7:29 and Mark 1:22 in regard to the authority of the Old Testament in Jesus' preaching.
10. How may the minister safeguard integrity in the ministry of the Word?

## Suggested Readings

Abbey, Merrill R. *Communication in Pulpit and Parish*. Philadelphia: The Westminster Press, 1973.

_____. *Preaching to the Contemporary Mind: Interpreting the Gospel Today*. Nashville: Abingdon Press, 1963.

Craddock, Fred B. *As One Without Authority*. Nashville: Abingdon Press, 1971.

_____. *Overhearing the Gospel*. Nashville: Abingdon Press, 1978.

Lewis, Ralph L. *Persuasive Preaching for Today*. Revised ed. Ann Arbor, Michigan: LithoCrafters, Inc., 1977.

McLaughlin, Raymond W. *The Ethics of Persuasive Preaching*. Grand Rapids: Baker Book House, 1979.

## Notes

1. Compare Acts 22:4-16; 26:9-18.
2. Dale Moody, *The Word of Truth* (Grand Rapids: William B. Eerdmans Publishing Company, 1981), pp. 105-106.
3. Jeffrey and Peterson, *Speech a Text with Adapted Reading*, 2nd ed. (New York: Harper and Row, 1975), p. 427 *ff*.
4. Ginger Szola, "Going Back to School," *Best Years* September-October 1983, p. 12.
5. George A. Buttrick, *Prayer* (New York: Abingdon-Cokesbury Press, 1942), p. 262.
6. Austin J. Freeley, *Argumentation and Debate*, 3rd ed. (Belmont, Calf.: Wadsworth Publishing Co., Inc. 1971), p. 142 *ff*. discusses the structure of argument. The model he attributes to Stephen Toulmin suggested the approach we have taken.

# 5
# The Inventive Basis of Preaching

God has given humans creative, inventive powers and has granted us a significant role in the process of sermon construction. The Spirit surely controls, but the Creator has endowed us with sensibility, the capacity to discern the truly meaningful. We have the privilege of determining the ideas which shall form our messages. This inventive task responds to the question: From where do sermons come? Generally a sermon begins with an idea or insight gained from Scripture or from the preacher's observation of life.

### Discovery of Sermon Ideas

Spiritual sensitivity is one of the best qualities a preacher can possess. Throughout his lifetime he should cultivate this quality. As a link between the ancient world of the Bible and the contemporary world, he bears responsibility to maintain an awareness of both worlds.

The cultivation of spiritual sensitivity can be accomplished partly through the pastoral activity of listening, hearing with a kind of sixth sense. As he listens, the minister develops a feel for the specific needs and wants of people. He will learn when emptiness occurs in life, where people need a word of help and instruction. The more he listens and learns, the more sensitive he becomes.

In addition, spiritual sensitivity can be developed through observation. The preacher observes life in general and people in particular. People give signals about themselves through the ways in which they act and interact with each other. The keen observer will learn much from those interactions. The pastor/preacher sees through the eyes of compassion and feels a special kind of love for his fellow humans. Beyond that, he knows that he bears a message for them from God which will address their deepest concerns.

Our pattern for this spiritual sensitivity is the Master Himself. He had compassion for the lost, the blind, the lame, the deaf, the lonely, and desperate people He met. He wept over the city of Jerusalem because of its sinfulness and wept when Lazarus, His friend, died. Jesus saw opportunities to bring a word from the Father on every occasion and in the life of every person He met. The preacher who remains sensitive will never lack for specific needs to address in sermons. Thus, the preacher discovers sermon ideas from people and events in all the world around him. He must be a student of human behavior, always sensitive to the need to bring his message from God to people.

Conversely, when he reads the Bible, the preacher senses the needs of his people. In its pages, he will find a wealth of truth involving humankind and God's dealings with us. Nothing will teach the preacher more about human nature than a regular, continuous program of Bible study. As he faithfully mines the Scripture, he will turn up one treasure after another which will eventually become sermons he may share with great delight.

One of the decisions the preacher should make early in his ministry relates to the retention of sermon ideas. First, he should write down every idea as it comes to him whether through contacts with people or through the reading of Scripture. Next, he should develop a method to retain these ideas. Ways to do this will vary from person to person. One good way is to keep the ideas in a loose-leaf notebook to facilitate classification under headings of interest. Another way is to keep them in a drawer of a desk at which he works on sermon preparation or in file folders arranged by topics.

However the minister chooses to store and retrieve ideas, he should read through them on a regular basis. Gordon Clinard, long-time preaching professor, referred to his retention of such ideas as a "sermon seedbed."[1] He followed the practice of looking through his idea file regularly to find ideas "growing" into future sermons. Those which did not appear to grow he would discard after a period of time. He recognized that some ideas, upon reflection, were not as worthy of development as he initially thought.

Now and then the diligent preacher will discover one idea while working on another or while searching for material to develop another idea. Something entirely different from what he expected will occur to him and demand immediate attention and development. This serendipitous discovery[2] will occasion excitement as the minister discovers evidence that God rewards those who faithfully study God's Word in order to find and declare truth.

Thus, sermon ideas come from pastoral contacts or from a regular program of Bible study. These are indirect or incidental ways of finding ideas for preaching.[3] The preacher should be aware of every possible source of sermon ideas. He does not necessarily go out hunting for sermonic material in all his contacts and reading. In fact, he should guard against the temptation to see a sermon in everything and everyone. On the other hand, he should be sensitive enough when something demands his attention to recognize its potential for a sermon.

## Discovery of Sermon Texts

The preacher also will have a regular program of Bible study during which time he specifically and purposefully searches for sermon texts. He will want a long-range plan which encompasses a number of short-term objectives. If he does not have both dimensions of planning, he may find himself forcing ideas into a text to achieve a short-term objective instead of allowing the text to speak to him through long-range development.

That minister who selects only those passages he likes best or the ones easiest to develop will be guilty of subjectivity which leads to a limited canon—preaching from only a few texts of Scripture. A revealing exercise is to review the texts from which you have preached over the last year. Do you discern a limitation of the canon based on your use of the Scriptures?

Count the number of sermons from the Old Testament and from the New. Consider the number of familiar passages and those less well known. Count as familiar those your listeners likely will recognize. Within the New Testament, list those from the Gospels, the Epistles of Paul, and the remainder of the New Testament. When you compile your data, you likely will find that there are three new Testament sermons for every one on an Old Testament text. In addition, within the New Testament you prefer either the Gospel material or the writings of Paul. Moreover, you will begin to discern that you preach on some favorite passages or books repeatedly and neglect others.

If, indeed, you do discover a problem, in what ways may you address it? First, seek a more objective method of text selection. The matter of text selection may be completely objective if you choose your texts from a lectionary, a recommended sequence of Scripture readings for every Sunday of the year, one of which may become the text for the sermon each Sunday.[4] The preacher does not have to belong to a liturgical tradition to consult the lectionary for suggestions for sermon texts. The ministers in the Free Church or Reformed tradition will recognize some of the seasons of the lectionary even if they are not familiar with all festivals and observances.

Use of the lectionary will have one overwhelming advantage for the preacher in his planning: It will help him range over the entire Bible in his selection of texts. A good way to discover the advantages to the lectionary is to consult it for help in planning the services after Thanksgiving through Easter. The passages are arranged to lead one through the two principal observances of the preaching year—Christmas and Easter.

To be sure, there is a disadvantage to this completely objective method of text selection: It may become mechanical and cause the minister to rely on someone else for sermon ideas and texts.

A second approach to solving the problem of a limited canon is to consciously practice selectivity. At times the minister may wish to employ the lectionary and at other times, to follow his own plan of arranging ideas and texts for preaching. He may prefer to design a lectionary of his own. Whatever your plan, attempt to include the contents of the entire Bible in your preaching. Avoid the practice of limiting the texts from which you preach.[5] You will be planning and preparing sermons for as long as you preach. Adopt and follow a thoughtfully devised, balanced plan of preaching.[6]

## Developing Sermon Topics

Once the minister has decided upon a series of texts, he should identify and develop topics from those texts. He must have a text and a subject for each sermon. For example, he may wish to speak about prayer from the experience of Jesus in Gethsemane (Matt. 26:36-46). To be more specific, he may limit the general idea of prayer to the subject of the necessity of prayer.

Those ideas which grow out of Bible study are well on their way toward development. Ideas or topics which originate outside the Scripture the minister should refine through texts, making certain each idea is expressed in Scripture before proceeding to develop a sermon on that topic.

Keep the following principles in mind as you develop sermon topics: First, be sensitive to divine leadership.

There is no procedure which may be substituted for the work of the Holy Spirit. The preacher must not forget the work of the Spirit or presume upon it by attempting to substitute "reliance upon the Spirit" for his own hard work in sermon development. The person who prepares sermons must seek and acknowledge the leadership of God throughout the preparation process.

In his relationships with the people of his congregation, the minister listens and interacts. He responds from within himself with love and understanding. He learns to read people through their words and actions and responds to them gently and confidently. That same kind of sensitivity also must apply to the Spirit's presence. The minister must know how to listen to and to follow the leading of the Spirit.

Second, allow time for growth. The process of preparation should include time to read the text slowly a number of times with no intent other than to listen to it and to find the direction of the Spirit in allowing the text to speak to the people. Of course, that meditative work cannot be hurried.

Jesus told the parable of the secretly growing seed to illustrate that growth takes time (Mark 4:26-29). Since sermon material needs time for maturation, the preacher should allow sufficient time in the process of sermon development for the maturing of his thoughts. There is no predetermined amount of time which will guarantee maturity. Some texts are simple and are quickly and easily understood. Other passages are more difficult and require more study and time for reflection.

It is probably impossible to complete an excellent sermon from the initial idea to final form in a matter of a day or two. As you move carefully through the procedures of sermon development, pray for guidance. Meditate on the text and listen for the Spirit's voice. Cultivate the material with repeated careful reading. Ask questions of the material. Determine whether the first thoughts about the text are correct and accurate. Does the passage really say what you think it does? Probing the material will serve to cultivate it and facilitate its growth.

Third, examine sermon topics in light of a highly developed cultural awareness. The minister is under obligation to understand two worlds: the ancient world of Scripture and the world of his congregation. Knowledge of the ancient world is enhanced through the study of commentaries and other sources which describe in detail the settings in which the Bible was written, the habits and customs of biblical persons, and the social and political factors of that world.

Awareness of the contemporary world requires that the preacher know the nature of its people and the social, political, and other forces which come to bear on them daily. He should become acquainted with the literature of the age and the influences for good and evil on the values and actions of people. This knowledge demands time for observation, interaction, and reflection.

### Developing the Sermon Affirmation

Building upon an understanding of the two worlds, biblical and contemporary, achieve a synthesis by combining the elements of the past and the present in a contemporary statement of affirmation for each sermon.

Ask: What do these worlds have in common? How do the people differ, and in what ways are they alike? What crises and capabilities to counter crisis do the inhabitants of the two worlds have in common? Determine the qualities of character and conduct common to all people. How are all people the same irrespective of their places in time and geography? State these answers in declarative sentences using the present tense. These concepts are timeless issues the preacher seeks to address in sermons. As an interpreter of the Bible, the minister is responsible for bringing the two worlds together through the speaking of the sermon.[7]

Once the preacher grasps the topics or themes of Scriptures and comprehends their application to persons of all generations, he understands clearly the importance of having each sermon make an affirmation. Affirming what the Bible affirms, saying what the Bible says, is preaching at its best. God's messenger desires to deliver to the congregation with conviction and power the truth of Scripture as affirmation. For example, an affirmation from the story of the Pharisee and the publican who went to the Temple to pray would be: Sincerity and humility are essential to prayer.

Frame the affirmation for each message and include its statement within your sermon notes or at the head of your manuscript. As you preach, allow your affirmation to serve as an indication of the extent to which you achieve your purpose.

## Identifying Sermon Intent

Idea, text, topic, and affirmation lead to the identification of an objective or purpose for preaching. This vital

*The Inventive Basis of Preaching* 111

step should not be overlooked: Upon it often hinges the success or failure of the sermon. The preacher should write out a controlling purpose for each sermon. The purpose is a statement of intent framed early in the preparation of the message and will serve the preacher by directing each step of development and presentation of the message. Each part of the sermon should serve the purpose—revealing it and leading toward the conclusion.

We have identified four categories of intent in preaching which shall assist us in framing our objectives.[8] They are, as follows: to inform, to stimulate, to convince, and to persuade. To frame the objective for a sermon, ask the following quesion: What do I intend for the hearer to know, recall, believe, or do through this sermon? Combine the response to that question with perceived characteristics of the congregation and the subject of the message. The result will be a statement similar to the following: My objective is to stimulate within the congregation through a retelling of the parable of the publican and the Pharisee the awareness that sincerity and humility are essential to prayer.

Without a specific objective in mind, the preacher risks aimlessness in his preaching. Have one idea in mind as you move toward the conclusion of each sermon and the invitation. The objective should guide presentation just as the affirmation keeps the content of the message before the preacher affording purposefulness and significance to proclamation.

Response to the gospel with belief is the ultimate goal of all proclamation. However, the preacher should have a specific response for each sermon as well, a response implicit in the intention and specific objective of that message. The minister desires for the listener to be, to do, or to believe something as a result of hearing the sermon. Refer to the objective suggested for Luke 18:9-14 (the Pharisee and the publican). A proper response to be sought in the sermon on prayer would be *that the listeners pray with sincerity and humility.* This example suggests a pattern for clarifying the responses sought in other types of sermons.

## Interpretation and Discovery of Meaning

The process of sermon preparation is not complete until the preacher correctly interprets the text from which he plans to preach. The task of interpretation is complex because it involves an ancient book and a modern world; it is necessary because our people need the message of the Bible.

Hermeneutics is the science of interpretation. We recommend that the minister develop his own method of interpretation incorporating the following components.[9]

*The Language Component.* This component includes three parts—the grammatical, the lexical, and the rhetorical or literary. Begin the study of grammar with sentences, the primary units of thought. Analyze the sentence construction of your text in the original, if possible. If you have no facility with Greek and Hebrew, do the exercise in English. Employ grammars, manuals, and the Bible in this work. Attempt to understand Hebrew and Greek grammar to acquire the ability to perceive thought patterns and meanings which are not apparent in English versions alone.

Lexical or word study demands discipline. Select a good lexicon to trace the etymology, history, and usage of words in your text. English lexicons and word studies offer help with this part of the study.

The rhetorical or literary component treats style and literary form of a text which also are vital to comprehension of meaning. Understanding figures of speech, individual mannerisms in expression, and idioms brings a passage to life.

*The Historical Component.* Our understanding of the Scripture is incomplete until we learn the historical setting of the text, its date and author, and the identity of its first readers. The manner in which God dealt with people at that time and place provides a key for understanding how he deals with us. Employment of the historical component will confirm for the interpreter that he stands in the stream of God's activity in human history, as did the biblical author, and gives the interpreter a perspective from which to speak eternal truth about God and his ways.

*The Theological Component.* Each interpreter should have an overarching theology of the Bible for the ability to see each sermon text as a part of the whole. Theology gives substance to the sermon, describes the activity of God in history, and discerns the manner in which he deals redemptively with humankind in all ages.

*The Comparative Component.* The comparative component is, at its simplest, the use of cross-references. It may be a comparison of two or more passages reporting the same event, as in the Synoptic Gospels, or the comments by two bibilical authors on the same subject, as Ephesians 2:8-9 and James 2:17-26 on faith. Its greatest value is that it permits the Bible to interpret itself. Also, it adds clarity and unity to sermons.

*The Homiletical Component.* The homiletical component is the restatement of the meaning of the text in the present tense. The term *homiletics* refers to the practice of preparing and delivering sermons, of bringing God's Word to humankind.

*The Spiritual Component.* The study of Scripture always should be under the tutelage of the Spirit. His work must come before, during, and after all human efforts in interpretation. This understanding pervades our approach to preaching.

In light of these components, we suggest the following procedure for discovery of the meaning of the text through interpretation.

1. Select the passage to be interpreted.
2. Read the passage many times in your favorite version.
3. Read the passage many times from other versions and, if possible, translate it from the original language.
4. As you are reading, write questions and impressions that may come to mind, but do not attempt to answer or expand upon your impressions during the reading process.
5. Prepare to study each verse of the text one sentence at a time. Devise a convenient method for recording your findings. Plan to write comprehensively since many of the concepts articulated at this stage may be refined for use in the sermon itself.
6. Using the available resources other than *commentaries*, research the passage, attempting to find

answers to issues raised, keeping in mind the hermeneutical components discussed previously. Remember to record your findings.
7. Write out an interpretative statement (one sentence) for each sentence in the passage.
8. Write out an interpretative statement for the entire passage. (This is the affirmation of the text.) If the passage is more than one paragraph, make a sentence for each paragraph and then one for the entire passage.
9. Consult several good commentaries and complete an exegesis of the passage.
10. Compare your findings (7. and 8.) with your exegetical work and reconcile the two in the interpretative statements.

Having completed the work of exegesis, the minister should review his sermon plan and compare the affirmation of the sermon with the affirmation of the text, making certain they are synonymous. Some revision of the sermon affirmation may be necessary after careful interpretation of the text.

Good interpretation leads to good preaching. Such interpretation demands thorough exegesis of the text as we attempt to ascertain its meaning through examination of lexicons, dictionaries, and commentaries. Discover the specific tools for biblical study and proper interpretation which are most helpful. The selection of sources is a matter of personal choice and conviction. There are, however, guidelines for employing them:

First, *be thorough in your study*. Interpretation requires completeness of study. Form, but do not accept, first impressions before testing them. If your first idea is correct, more investigation will not discredit it. For example, in Judges 9:7-15 we read that the trees talked to each other. Careful study of the passage reveals that these talking trees appear in a parable told by Jotham to describe the actions of the Israelites in their choice of Abimelech as their king.

The Bible contains various kinds of literature, some of which employ figurative language. To accept a literal interpretation in, for example, a parable would be to miss the truth presented in parabolic form. A simple understanding of parable is a story told to convey meaning other than its literal one. Careful, comprehensive study will examine the words of the text and the form of literary expression. Be thorough in your approach to the discovery of meaning.

Second, *maintain a systematic approach to interpretation.* Follow a topic, name, theme, or doctrine throughout the entire Bible. For example, the name of God appears in Genesis 1:1. To learn about God, trace the name of God as it is employed from Genesis through Revelation. Refer only to those passages which mention God. When you have reached the final book in the Bible, you will have formulated a systematic approach to understanding the Bible's teachings about God.

There is benefit in a comprehensive, systematic plan of study for it will afford verification of the principles which we form into sermons. Internal consistency ought to be easy to achieve through careful procedures in sermon preparation. But the demand is more exacting than that: We must be consistent message to message. Everything we say for God should validate and confirm every other statement we make for Him. We are not always careful enough. The conscientious listener may be confused when we, for example, preach upon the love of God in one message and in another upon the wrath of God. The apparent contradiction may be addressed through an understanding which comes to us from systematic theology. God's wrath is the other side of His love. Continuous rejection of God's love will bring the sinner the wrath of God. Thus, God's wrath is love's rejection of the rejection of love. Systematic study will result in consistent content in preaching.

Third, *permit the Spirit to guide*. We have stressed the role of the Spirit in every phase of preparation to preach. To exclude the Spirit's presence and insight from our interpretation would be a serious lapse. The Spirit as teacher enables the mystery of redemption to be both grasped and understood. The deep things of God which will enrich our preaching can only be known through openness to the Spirit's leading as we plumb the depths of the Scriptures. The role of the Spirit in inspiration secures the Spirit's role in interpretation.

The person who searches the Scripture consistently, studies thoroughly and systematically under the Spirit's leadership with a view to understanding it will experience the joy of discovery. That joy cannot come by adopting in toto what others have said about the Bible without investigating its meaning for yourself. Neither can it come by parroting what others have said in their sermons without any effort of your own. The joy of discovery comes only through making the search; your efforts bear rich rewards for you and those to whom you preach.

Indeed, the minister who proclaims God's Word has the responsibility to read it and find for himself the great truths of the Bible. When he makes his own discovery, confirms that discovery by the findings of others, and builds his sermons on the basis of it, he finds an excitement in preparing, as well as in proclaiming.

Therefore, when he comes before his people, the preacher can declare: "Thus, saith the Lord" and proceed to bring the message with a sense of confidence and urgency in his preaching; he will speak with an authority born from the conviction that he does not bring his own thoughts, untested and unconfirmed; he brings God's Word.

### Making the Meaning Clear

The preacher employs illustrations to help make his meaning clear. The basic definition of the verb *to illustrate* is "to enlighten or illuminate." Of the techniques available to the preacher to help make himself understood, illustration of truth is perhaps the most compelling.

The average listener in today's congregation cannot always comprehend the preacher's explanations, applications, and argument. That places a greater responsibility on the preacher to strive for clarity. He must choose images, stories, points of contrast, and comparison from the world in which we live to establish for his listeners the points of reference to enable them to grasp biblical and theological concepts. The minister explains something they do not understand by referring to something they do understand and pointing out the similarities.

## The Inventive Basis of Preaching

While illustration may be understood as support for the sermon and, thus, a part of the logical basis of preaching,[10] the discovery of illustrative material occupies much of the inventive work of sermon preparation. The sources to which we may turn for illustrations are not unlike those employed to discover sermon topics or to enrich the store of general knowledge the preacher must cultivate. The inventive task of illustration discovery points us to specific sources which include the following:
1. The Bible
2. Nonbiblical literature
3. Observation of life
4. The minister's vocation

### The Bible

The preacher will turn often to the Scriptures for illustrations. Its narratives, poetry, character studies, explanations, and figures of speech illuminate our development of the themes of faith. The fact that they are often well known does not diminish their impact. Christians have a profound appreciation of the Bible. Use of biblical material strikes a responsive note, even though it is familiar. Biblical writers themselves drew on the contents of the Bible as they wrote. Paul referred to Abraham as an illustration of justification (Rom. 4:1-25). Jesus pointed out the sinfulness of Noah's generation when he spoke of the conditions of the world before his return (Matt. 24:37 *ff.*). The writer of the Epistle to the Hebrews revealed comprehensive understanding of Old Testament events and transformed these into metaphors to foster understandings of the Christ event.

## Nonbiblical Literature

A second source for finding illustrations is nonbiblical literature. History, for example, is filled with stories of people of courage and commitment to faith. Poets across the ages have recorded impressions of reality similar to those of David and the other psalmists. The romantic idealism of the Song of Solomon has been voiced repeatedly throughout history. The history of the church also provides a vast storehouse of illustrations. Men and women of faith through time serve as noble examples of the power of Christ's working in lives. Names like John Wycliffe, John Bunyan, Roger Williams, Ann and Adoniram Judson, Ida Scudder, Lottie Moon, Bill Wallace, Rebekah Naylor, and others quickly bring to mind the depth of devotion required of God's people in difficult times.

A program of reading in a wide variety of types of literature will enable the preacher to discover an amazing number of ways to provide light in his sermons.

## Observation of Life

We have already advocated the cultivation of sensitivity to persons, relationships, and events as a source for sermon ideas. Observation of life about him offers the minister a wealth of illustrative material. The minister is often the one observed. His prominent role in the life of the church and of his community may dissuade him from direct, objective encounter with life about him. While anonymity may be impossible in the community where he ministers, and the adjustment in behavior to the presence of "the reverend" may be unavoidable, the preacher needs to cultivate acceptance and honest response in order to locate the pulse of the community of which he is a part. Association with nonchurch community groups engaged in worthwhile endeavors allows the minister a vantage point for observing life about him which can be helpful in the successful quest for illustrations. Again, such activity will aid the pastor's achieving balance in his personal and professional life.

**The Minister's Vocation**

The nature of the pastoral work is such that the pastor constantly will come into contact with fellow human beings from whom he can learn. People are interested in other people, as attested by the amazing popularity of people-oriented magazines, gossip columns, and human interest stories. When illustrations are drawn from life as the pastor observes it in his exercise of his pastoral duties, interest and responsiveness by the congregation are both high.

Hospital visits, for example, provide the pastor with numerous testimonies to faith and courage which may be shared gladly with others. The same may be said of visits to retirement homes, extended-care facilities, or the private homes of those who no longer can be active in church and society because of confining illnesses. Such illustrations aid our understanding of biblical passages which speak of the Christian life (Matt. 5:14-16) and instruct us to maintain our faith and loyalty to Christ in spite of all difficulty (Phil. 4:11; 2 Cor. 4:8 *ff.*).

Let ideas for illustration grow naturally out of the daily give and take of life. Remember one of the basic rules expressed earlier. As you study the Bible, keep your people in mind. As you contact your people, keep the Bible in mind. The preacher is a participant in life with the congregation. At the same time, he is a student of the Word and a messenger speaking that Word of God.

**Use of Illustrations**

Finding, recording, and employing good illustrations is a never-ending challenge for the preacher. Once he has developed a satisfactory plan for discovering and filing them, he should work toward the effective use of illustrations in the sermon. We offer the following suggestions.

1. An illustration should make the point. Keep firmly in mind the idea which you seek to clarify. Avoid the practice of amplifying a detail which will detract from the point. If you lose track of your own thoughts, what will the listener do?
2. An illustration should be necessary. Resist the temptation to illustrate the obvious and neglect the obscure.
3. Watch for abstract terms. Illustrate to give more tangible evidence of complex ideas.
4. Employ illustrations to verify those facts which may be difficult to accept (judgment, for example).
5. Restate ideas of surpassing excellence through illustration. The majesty of God is one such idea.
6. Make certain you understand the significance of the details of the illustrations you employ and that the details are correct. Using spelling pronunciation one preacher referred to the "Mag-i-not Line" of defense. It was apparent he hadn't the vaguest notion what it was. Another made a brief reference

to "King Hamlet," an office the disturbed Dane never occupied.
7. Finally, the illustrations which are yours are strongest. If you form the habit of finding and writing your own material, you will understand the details, know their validity, and express them confidently. Should you employ the material of others, acknowledge your debt. Check the documentation provided by those you quote. Know and trust the writers upon whom you rely for secondary information.

The best illustrations are those which seem natural and maintain the unity and continuity of the message. Since illustrations are among the most memorable parts of a sermon, seek them aggressively as you read and minister, be selective in their use, and present them as stories with life-changing potential.

## Think on These Things

1. List the sources of sermon ideas in order from most significant to least significant. Justify your order.
2. Clip from the newspaper one human interest article every day for a week. Categorize them by subjects. Find a biblical text each one of them would help to clarify. Mount each on an 8½-by-11-inch sheet of paper for ease in identification and filing.
3. Find examples of the following literary types in the Bible: history, drama, poetry, and first-person narrative.
4. Identify the following passages by genre:
    a. Genesis 22:1-19
    b. Daniel 7

c. Luke 10:25-37
   d. Matthew 25:1-13
   e. Revelation 4:1-11
5. Construct a step-by-step procedure to follow in biblical interpretation.
6. Note fresh perspectives you gain from reading Romans 5:12-21 from five different *translations* of the Bible.
7. Develop an illustration file for upcoming sermons. Seek interesting and relevant illustrations for the messages. Use varied sources. Identify one excellent illustration for each of four sermons you plan to preach. What makes each exceptional?

## Suggested Readings

Adams, Jay E. *Preaching with Purpose: A Comprehensive Textbook on Biblical Preaching.* Grand Rapids: Baker Book House, 1982.

Aycock, Don M., Ed. *Preaching with Purpose and Power: Selected E. Y. Mullins Lectures on Preaching.* Macon, Ga.: Mercer University Press, 1982.

Best, Ernest. *From Text to Sermon: Responsible Use of the New Testament in Preaching.* Atlanta: John Knox Press, 1964.

Macpherson, Ian. *The Art of Illustrating Sermons.* Nashville: Abingdon Press, 1964.

Sangster, W. E. *The Craft of Sermon Illustration.* Philadelphia: The Westminster Press, 1950.

Steel, David. *Preaching Through the Year.* Atlanta: John Knox Press, 1980.

Von Rad, Gerhard. *Biblical Interpretations in Preaching.* Translated by John E. Steely. Nashville: Abingdon, 1977.

# The Inventive Basis of Preaching

## Notes

1. The late Gordon Clinard served as professor of preaching at Southwestern Baptist Theological Seminary in Fort Worth, Texas, from 1955 to 1966. The ideas in this paragraph came from his classroom lecture notes.
2. This idea comes from a discussion by James W. Cox in *A Guide to Biblical Preaching* (Nashville: Abingdon, 1976), pp. 46-48.
3. See Gary Stratman, *Pastoral Preaching: Timeless Truth for Changing Needs* (Nashville: Abingdon Press, 1983), pp. 55-60.
4. For more information on the lectionary, see Cox, appendix C, pp. 129-38.
5. See James D. Smart, *The Strange Silence of the Bible in the Church: A Study in Hermeneutics* (Philadelphia: The Westminster Press, 1971). Smart says: "The voice of the Scriptures is falling silent in the preaching and teaching of the church and in the consciousness of Christian people," (p. 15). He suggests that part of the problem lies with the preacher, who is not exposing people to enough Scripture. This is a problem which can be corrected, in part, from the pulpit.
6. A planned program of preaching is a list of sermon ideas and texts prepared for a specified number of worship services in advance. For the minister attempting his first one, a three-month plan is a good way to begin. See J. Winston Pearce, *Planning Your Preaching* (Nashville: Broadman Press, 1967), for a guide.
7. John R. W. Stott, *Between Two Worlds: The Art of Preaching in the Twentieth Century* (Grand Rapids: William B. Eerdmans Publishing Company, 1982), p. 137, refers to this as "bridge-building."
8. In chapter 4, "The Logical Basis."
9. These components are summaries of principles of interpretation found in L. Berkhof, *Principles of Biblical Interpretation* (Grand Rapids: Baker Book House, 1950); Clinton Lockhart, *Principles of Interpretation* (Kansas City, Kan.: Central Seminary Press, 1950: A. Berkeley Mickelsen, *Interpreting the Bible* (Grand Rapids: William B. Eerdmans, 1963); and Bernard Ramm *Protestant Biblical Interpretation: A Textbook of Hermeneutics*, 3rd revised ed. (Grand Rapids: Baker Book House, 1970). For a summary of principles of interpretation for preaching see William D. Thompson, *Preaching Biblically: Exegesis and Interpretation*, The Abingdon Preacher's Library, ed. William D. Thompson, (Nashville: Abingdon, 1981), pp. 45-77.
10. See chapter 4, "The Logical Basis."

# 6

## The Ideational Basis of Preaching

The indictment was severe: "My preacher hasn't read a book of substance since he left seminary. He seems to get his ideas for sermons from old books of illustrations which he doesn't even update. He'll describe a man's coming into town on the train, taking his valise, and walking to the hotel. That when there isn't a passenger train in our state, nobody has a 'valise,' much less carries one, and you wouldn't dare walk to the hotel in a strange city."

The ideational basis of preaching addresses this problem: Through what means does the preacher apprehend and nurture the ideas which will ultimately become sermons? *Ideational* is the adjectival form of the verb, ideate: to form *in idea, thought, or imagination*. The ideational basis of preaching, then, is the process by which the preacher adds to the store of his understandings and insights. It is at one and the same time *sensitivity* which enables him to recognize the worth of ideas and *acumen*, intellectual ability, to retain them until they are needed.

Our preaching ideas are incomplete until they have been fully expressed in a sermon. For the idea to grow to maturity, time and cultivation are essential. The minister who desires to be fresh and appealing in his preaching will consciously seek new ideas, nurture their development to maturity, and find the best means to express them sermonically as he meets the goals he imposes upon himself in his planned preaching program.

We will be tempted to preach ideas before they have matured. The scramble is upon us after all for next Sunday. The temptation is to remove the plant from the soil when it has barely sprouted to enter it in the flower show. The judges will be confused and suspicious of our gardening skills. This chapter seeks to help the preacher select the seed, nurture development, and pick the bloom at its peak of beauty and perfection.

## The Spiritual Dimension

Ours is a task of the mind, to be sure, and of the Spirit. There is no conflict here. We seek ideas for sermons among the widest interests of our lives. As ministers we may not ignore the spiritual dimension among these interests since they breathe life and significance into the verbal expression of our messages. The work of preparing sermons is not a mechanical routine which, when mastered, can be employed to produce sermons automatically. The spiritual aspect of our task enriches the procedures we follow. Indeed, without cultivation of the spiritual dimension of his life and ministry, the minister's sermons may be little more than good advice or organized opinion on moral questions or Bible times, persons, and events.

Indeed, preachers should back away from the regimen of searching for and studying texts solely for the preparation of sermons. The text is not to be "used" or "manipulated." The new hermeneutic taught us that the text, the Word, interprets us as we interpret the Word.[1] We stand under the text and allow it to judge us. Only when the interaction and dialogue with the text are complete are we ready to preach. The spirit of the text becomes the spirit of the preacher.

What we exhort others to do we must accept as our obligation as well: We must set aside time for devotional reading of the Bible, prayer, meditation, and reflection. This is a prescription for the health of our spirit. Beyond that, a devotional regimen will enable the preacher to confront significant ideas which may become the genesis of sermons.

First, we stress the importance of devotional study. We preachers too easily develop habits of studying the Bible for only one purpose: It is the place where we get our texts for next Sunday's sermons. For the Bible to have full value, the minister should practice reading and studying it devotionally. The preacher, like other Christians, needs nourishment for his soul. To neglect devotional practices from the pressures of other activity or upon the assumption that an adequate substitute may exist in other good work is to lose a vital source of spiritual health.

Select a book of the Bible from which you plan no sermons for the next three months. Read from it and take notes every day. Pick a time and a place outside the study. Let this be in addition to the readings done with your family during the devotional time with them. Allot yourself enough time to read a chapter or more from your favorite translation. Then compare it with other

## The Ideational Basis of Preaching

translations you have. Seek a full understanding of the passage and try to determine its specific application to *you* as a Christian person. Have no other thought in mind except the worth of the Scripture to your own life. This practice which we commend to others is a worthy one for us as well.

Devotional books on biblical topics also can provide inspiration.[2] In addition to the biblical material, read some in one of these each day. Read until a thought strikes you as applicable to your experience and needs. Or, read a defined unit such as a chapter each day to strengthen your spirit. Biographies of well-known Christians are easy to read and are a source of profound encouragement for the Christian. Do not ignore devotional classics, such as Augustine's *Confessions*, Bunyan's *The Pilgrim's Progress, Foxe's Book of Martyrs*, and primary sources from church history. Major denominations publish devotional guides and prayer calendars which will add greatly to the values derived from the study of Scripture when they are read consistently and thoughtfully.

Second, consider the importance of prayer. Of course the preacher will pray for guidance in the preparation of every sermon. Yet, the preacher also needs in all of life the strength derived from prayer for direction, for God's will to be done. He should pray for his family and each member, for his country and its leadership, for wisdom to function well in society at large. A study of the lives of outstanding preachers reveals that they were men of prayer and devotion. They guarded their devotional time carefully.

Sermon study notes also need prayer as they begin to

take shape in the form of sermons. The tasks of biblical interpretation and sermon preparation require great dependence on the Spirit's leadership. It is an awesome responsibility to go before the congregation to declare God's word. Proclamation presumes understanding. Let us diligently work and seriously pray for that understanding, then stand and proclaim the Word confidently and boldly.

Third, practice meditation and reflection. Our mad rush through the days has all but robbed us of the art of meditation. The psalmist declared that a righteous man meditates day and night on God's law (Ps. 1:2). To have time for meditation the preacher will have to set aside a period to be held inviolate from other demands in a hectic and pressure-filled schedule. That discipline is essential. Meditation may not be hurried. It requires that one close one's eyes and give free flight to one's thoughts on a given passage or concept. The mind will explore all the depth, height, and breadth of an idea. The name of God, the excellencies of God captured the imagination of the psalmist: "O Lord, our Lord, how excellent is thy name in all the earth" (Ps. 8:1, KJV). That happy declaration, no doubt, grew out of meditation. In fact, the very language of the psalm suggests meditation: "When I consider thy heavens . . ." (v. 3).

Ideas for sermon development spring from meditation. Consider the portion of a devotional passage or unit of study as a text for a given sermon. Ask yourself: What does it mean for life if (since) this word is true? The answer may serve as a key to the plan for the sermon. Again, consider this question about the text: What are all the implications of this truth? Allow the mind and spirit to mull over text, context, and life. Your answers may suggest the application of the text to your life needs and thence to the hurts of your congregation.

Reflection is a look backward. Once the preacher has read an entire chapter or book, there is great value in thinking through the context of the passage and seeking to understand the setting in which it is located. This work should be done with reference to your notes and underlining but not to commentaries, dictionaries, or other sources. Let yourself be a participant in the actual events of the text. When the interpreter lives with Scripture and becomes a part of it, he will feel the movement of events, see the places, listen to the sounds, and interact emotionally with the biblical personalities. This participation will strengthen the devotional life and eventually deepen the insight preached from the pulpit.

The preacher constantly goes to the Scripture in search of something to say. The attendant risk is that he will refer to the Bible only for a text for the next sermon. Constantly guard against the temptation to neglect your devotional life. Read for God's message to you. Pray always for yourself and those to whom you minister. Learn the art of meditation and reflection. Your personal maturity will enrich your experience and become apparent in the pulpit to those who listen to you week by week.

## Understanding the Contemporary Context for Proclamation

Having established a plan for personal Bible study, the preacher will need to turn his attention to the world in which he lives and serves. The study of Scripture acquaints him with the ancient world of the Old and New Testaments. His knowledge is incomplete, however, until he also becomes conversant with the world in the present. The context for our ministry is complex. Attempt to remain abreast of current events, study the role of the church in the world, and aggressively seek the most effective ways to live in the world without completely identifying with it.

First, cultivate your comprehension of contemporary events. No preacher can minister effectively who is unaware of the events which shape and influence the lives of contemporary people. We have arrived at Huxley's Brave New World. Our people are confused and confounded by the rapid movement of history. Technology advances faster than technicians can keep up with it. Instant communication is taken for granted. We have no difficulty today with access to information. On all fronts humankind seems to be advancing at an alarming rate.

In the midst of all this, the preacher stands with his Bible, seeking to solve the problems of humanity. Without a broad comprehension of this world, the preacher will be at a loss to know how to speak the necessary word of God. This is no mandate for the preacher to become a person of the world: Instead it is a reminder to the preacher to learn about culture and people in order to know how to communicate more effectively the word of God.

Cultivation of an understanding of the contemporary setting for ministry requires great sensitivity on the part of the preacher. He should become acquainted with the fears and hopes of his congregants. He needs to know

## The Ideational Basis of Preaching

the factors which influence their decisions. Do they have interest in world peace, world hunger, or world health? Do they follow events in the Middle East? in Latin America? behind the Iron Curtain? across the state line? at the city council meeting?

A good self-test will help you to measure your own awareness. Make a list of the current events which affect the lives of your people. Put down from your general knowledge every possible person, event, and trend which comes to mind. Then ask yourself how much you personally know about each one. Speak impromptu on each area of concern. Are you coherent? Can you supply details to support attitudes you express? Are the names of those responsible for decision making known to you? Further, jot down some preliminary ways in which you may address the concerns of your people and suggest biblical texts which are relevant. You probably will find many preaching possibilities: Nuclear annihilation, polluted air, insufficient income, terminal illness, family pressures, insecurity, and others are legitimate concerns which the preacher can address from the Word of God. When you begin to preach from a consciousness of such contemporary concerns, you will find an upturn in the amount of interest people give to your sermons. Your awareness of their interests and needs will stem from careful observation of current events.

A caution must be expressed: The preacher cannot become an instant expert by reading a single news article or editorial. Issues are often complex. The discipline required to read comprehensively and evaluatively to grasp issues, to put them in a framework to afford perspective, and to discern their significance is time consuming and demands thoughtful, objective analysis. The minister should seek among the many that could be studied those that *require* a word from the Scripture or the attention of the Christian community. He must pay the price to gain the knowledge essential for dealing with these issues from a biblical (moral, ethical) point of view.

We recommend consistent use of the following sources of information to aid the preacher in his understanding of contemporary concerns.

1. Read the local newspaper *carefully*. It is imperative that the minister know what his congregants are reading, pondering, and discussing. Even if the newspaper is not a comprehensive daily record of the city's life, it should not be ignored.
2. Read one comprehensive (regional) newspaper daily. Evaluate the editorial policy of the newspaper. Discover the biases that color its presentation of news and opinion. Seek to read as unbiased a news source as is available to you. You may need to consider subscribing to a good newspaper by mail, perhaps the Sunday edition only.
3. Consistently sample nonprint media in the same way. Local and national television and radio news programs should receive attention. Be conscious of the biases present here as well.
4. A newsmagazine or two may be selected in much the same way: Seek comprehensive objective presentation and analysis of national and international events. Your reading program is sufficiently comprehensive when you find yourself rereading essentially the same information in more than one source.

5. Your church may have an office, agency, or commission assigned responsibility for analysis of news and the compilation of data on social, political, or moral issues. Careful utilization of such materials is an essential balance to analyses that are essentially secular in nature.
6. Identify discussion groups in your community or church which focus upon contemporary concerns. Encourage and participate in such endeavors.
7. Keep your Bible handy as you survey contemporary issues or concerns. Allow its timeless truths to speak to timely matters. Note relevant and related passages.

The minister and the church, however, are to do more than become acquainted with the world; they are to speak the relevant word from God to the world. The Old Testament prophet Amos responded to God's call. He went to the capital of the Northern Kingdom to preach. There he saw social, political, and personal corruption on a grand scale. Amos stood and fearlessly proclaimed God's demands for justice and righteousness. He called for reforms, beginning with worship in the Temple. He indicted interrelationships among God's own people. Amos did not stop there: God's message was addressed to society at large as well. At great personal risk, he condemned the habits of the rich and powerful, including those who held civil authority.

Amos serves as an example for the preacher who brings a word of judgment to contemporary culture. The role of the church in today's society is the same it has always been: We are to bring a message of redemption to the world.

In some quarters the church has retreated. It has become no more than a sounding board for the latest religious trends. The preacher in such a church becomes a spokesman for somebody else or everybody else. Amplifying what others say, he abandons his own convictions or refuses to shape them for himself and merely reflects the ideas of others. The church which becomes a sounding board risks the loss of its own identity. It drifts toward lifelessness and soon appears to have little integrity and spiritual vitality.

In other places, the church has become merely an echo, reverberating sounds which originate elsewhere. The church as echo has no function other then repetition of someone else's message. The preacher becomes a mirror, reflecting what he sees and a parrot, repeating what he hears. The church and the minister relinquish the prophetic thrust of their ministry. They have no judgments to make, no reforms to initiate. Redemption no longer remains as a possibility. They will shortly become just one more voice in a world filled with cacophony.

But another possibility exists for the church: It may become a tone, a clear, resonant voice in the world, sounding out the gospel message. According to 1 Thessalonians 1 the church at Thessalonica must have been such a voice. Everywhere Paul went he heard about their testimony. Indeed the New Testament church set the tone for all time. Preach the lordship of Christ. Call for repentance and belief in the living Christ. Stand in judgment over the sin of the world. The voice of Simon Peter has never been silenced. "We must obey God rather than men" (Acts 5:29). "Repent and be baptized"

(Acts 2:38). "There is no other name . . . by which we must be saved" (Acts 4:12). The message of the risen Lord is *the* message. He came to establish life and righteousness for all time.

The responsibility of the individual Christian and of the church is to *be in the world* but *not of the world*. That was the prayer of Jesus in his high priestly prayer (John 17). We are residents of the world: Here we preach and serve. Our choices range from complete identity with the world (in which case we have no message) to total separation from the world (in which case we lose our voice). The Christian minister must participate in culture enough to know how to address it but must not identify so completely with culture that he cannot bring a word of redemption to it.

## Enriching the Content of Preaching Through General Reading

Knowledge of culture can be gained, in part, through reading from a wide variety of published works. Every preacher should have a program of general reading. In that reading, he will come into contact with his culture and learn something about its values, traditions, trends, and its people. To gain the greatest benefit, the preacher should identify several areas and read something in each of the areas on a regular basis.[3] Areas from which to select include current events, history, literary classics, fiction, nonfiction, technology, politics, the arts, and biographical works. No one can expect to stay current in all areas, but a plan of reading some from each of these areas on a regular schedule will enrich the content of preaching.

One respected minister in our acquaintance feared that his contact with the world of ideas would suffer from the administrative and pastoral duties inherent in his vocation. To counter that danger, he purchased the *Harvard Classics* and began a program of reading—*lectio continua*. He maintained that the resultant contact with significant ideas enriched his store of knowledge and positively affected his sermon development through the years.

From time to time publishers develop programs for providing the public with collections of significant literary works. A set such as the *Great Books* should be more than visually impressive upon the minister's bookshelves. They should be read. The retention of college literature textbooks and anthologies may represent subconscious awareness that the initial reading under the duress of assignment had been hurried and superficial. Reading from these for contact with significant writers has undoubtedly been postponed long enough.

The minister must not exclude from his reading program the work of twentieth-century poets. While he may not find a series of rhymed couplets to conclude a sermon structured of three points, he will discover that the poet deals profoundly with the significant concerns of contemporary culture. Faith pervades the writings of the Anglican T. S. Eliot or the Catholic Gerard Manly Hopkins. The insights of William Carlos Williams or Wallace Stevens may seem informed by another, less familiar philosophical approach to issues of our age. Nevertheless the poet teaches economy of language—a lesson all need. He also speaks from a mind informed by deep feeling—a desirable model for the minister.

## The Ideational Basis of Preaching

Enrichment in our preaching may be perceived by our hearers through fresh, interesting, and factual illustrations. The preacher who reads from numerous sources will have an exciting variety of them. Listeners can understand events about which they, too, have read in the latest newsmagazine or newspaper. They can identify with people about whom they hear and from whom they read on a regular basis. The sermon supporting material gathered by the preacher from wide reading will dramatically increase the interest value of his preaching.

A well-designed program of general reading can assist the minister through the improvement of *style*. Daily reading will bring the preacher into contact with material written by professionals. News writers must pack the most information into the fewest words. They must write understandably and, at the same time, say everything required with accuracy and economy of language.

Writers whose efforts enjoy the refinement possible when publishing deadlines are not immediate may affect our *style* in writing as well. In novels and biographies, the preacher reads long, detailed narratives and character descriptions. The novelist pays attention to detail. The biographer gives insight into personality. A diligent student of style in literature will find significant clues to improve one's own writing ability. Recognizing the constraints inevitable in the busy minister's schedule, we suggest the reading of short stories as another literary form which can aid the preacher. An excellent writer, such as John Cheever or Flannery O'Connor, may afford good insight into human situations and characters. At the same time, the writer may serve as a model for handling narrative elements in the condensed framework of the short story, a form analagous to the narrative sermon or the extended illustration. Preachers who wish to improve their style should study the works of those who are recognized for good writing. Beyond that, the secret to improvement is to practice what you already know.

Also, we shall enrich our sermons through the personal element injected into our messages. The preacher who reads knows the human condition. When he stands to preach, the listeners become aware that the sermon is about their predicament. Sadly, some hearers already have decided that preachers speak in broad generalities about the long ago; they dismiss us as pitiable people who perform our duty by preaching. What's more, they fulfill their duty by coming to listen to us preach, but our words do not mean much to them.[4] A key to the resolution of this dilemma is in our conscientiousness in general reading to inform our sermons with common ground and uncommon insight.

## Enriching the Content of Preaching through Biblical and Theological Study

Indeed, the uncommon character of our proclamation comes from a companion area of reading in the specific areas of our interest which demand attention—the biblical and the theological. In this age of specialization, the minister is a specialist in these two areas. In them his knowledge must be extensive. No reading plan has proper balance unless significant time is given to the fields of the preacher's particular interests.

## The Ideational Basis of Preaching

We have already stressed the importance of devotional reading of the Bible for personal enrichment. Now we turn attention to the in-depth study of the language, structure, and history of the biblical text. For that the preacher will need concordances, lexicons, grammars, and similar technical books. Recent scholarship has produced study aids of great value to the preacher. The number of Bible translations alone which have appeared over the past twenty years is astonishing. A mere comparison of translations and versions no longer is a simple task. Other indications of the fruit of biblical scholarship abound—word study books, dictionaries of Old and New Testament words, and new commentaries.

Sermon content can be enriched through proper use of contemporary biblical scholarship. For example, a preacher may cite the same verse in several Bible translations to clarify meaning. The believer's struggle with evil which Paul discussed in the latter part of Romans 7 may be cited as an example. A quick reading through the King James Version will not suffice for a clear understanding of the intent. Comparative readings, though, do enable the reader to comprehend better the battle Paul had with evil. Comparison of translations is one simple step into more extensive biblical study. Its value to the preacher and the listener will be evident.

The study of the findings of biblical scholarship should not send preachers to pulpits with long, arduous technical discussions. We study in order to undergird the biblical authority of sermons. We maintain an awareness of scholarly work in order to gain the confidence of our hearers in the trustworthiness of our words. If the trumpet makes an uncertain sound, the troops will not rally.

One of the basic assumptions of this book is that the preacher is a theologian or ought to be. As you stand before the people week after week with your proclamations, you are giving them your theology. Most, if not all, of the theology the listeners get they will receive from you. Theological study is not an option for the preacher; it is a necessity. One of the greatest benefits from recent studies in preaching has been the renewed emphasis on theology.[5]

Begin with a study of systematic theology. It will give strength to your sermons by verifying, validating, or correcting your own convictions. When the inevitable occurs and one of your convictions seems wrong, you will have a way of testing that conviction. A failure to find agreement among numerous theologians is no indication that you are wrong. Conversely, it is no confirmation that you are right. Acquire and develop the habit of reading a thorough systematic work with all your other reading. With all your books, you may not be able to pick one up and read through it before you start on another. That will severely limit the number of works you finish. Keep several books going simultaneously. Read a little from four or five in a day instead of reading long periods of time in one large book. One-volume systematics will get you off to a good start on systematic theology. Then, pursue areas of particular interest with specialized volumes. Old Testament and New Testament theologies should be the next step beyond general works.[6]

## The Imperative to Listen Sermonically

Everything the preacher does ultimately becomes a part of sermon preparation. He develops a certain posture toward life by virtue of his role and position as a minister. He "listens" to everything "sermonically." By that we mean that he sees potential in everything for a sermon.

First, the preacher listens to others. His interest is not mere curiosity. He listens for the concerns, problems, and other human factors which he may address with a word from God. As a student of human behavior, the preacher knows that if he listens closely enough people will tell about themselves.

Perhaps nothing helps more with listening than the role of pastor. In most traditions, the minister is considered a pastor first of all and then a preacher. As a pastor the minister will have contacts with people who need counseling. Much counseling is listening. The kind of listening you learn to do as a pastor will assist in developing the skill of hearing what people are really saying.

While he will never violate confidence in his sermons, he will wish to address the common problems of humankind in his sermons. Doubt, fear, insecurity, guilt, anxiety, sorrow, and loneliness are common to all of us. He who listens discovers that people are crying for help. If they do not get it from the pulpit, where will they get it?[7]

Second, the preacher hears his own sermons. It is impossible for the preacher to hear himself as others hear him, but he should listen as one who also stands under the gospel. We are not exempt from the Word we preach to everyone else. If we consider ourselves above and beyond the requirements of the Word, it will soon become obvious to the listeners. They, in turn, will soon cry: "Physician, heal thyself." In your preaching make it clear that all, including the preacher, are equal before God. His standards of life and righteousness are the same for all. Hypocrisy in one pulpit affects preachers in all pulpits. Learn to listen as one who needs the message. In reality you do.

Hearing your own sermons enables you to empathize with the others who hear you. They want to know that we understand and love them. Also, they are more likely to repond to our preachments if they know we have accepted for our own lives what we offer to them.

Third, and above all else, the preacher is attuned to the Spirit. Listen always for His voice. He will be your teacher throughout the entire process of sermon preparation and delivery. Nowhere in preaching should we presume upon the role of the Spirit. He is the Spirit of truth; He dwells with you and shall be in you (John 14:17). He is your guide; He will guide you into all truth (John 16:13). Depend on the Spirit for understanding and direction as you prepare. God, who has called you to speak His Word, will enable you to preach. As you read, pray, meditate, reflect, and write, listen for the instruction of the Spirit. The truth He tells is the truth you must proclaim, for it is God's truth.

Our listening, our biblical and theological study, our general reading, and our devotional activities combine with all elements of our vocation to add to the store of ideas we shall depend upon for the development of

# The Ideational Basis of Preaching

messages (sermons). Sooner or later we shall find ourselves in the pulpit preaching a carefully prepared message when a fresh insight, inspired by the Spirit, will come to us. The completeness of its form and its rightness for the moment will astonish us. The Spirit of God will have sought within our spirit for that word. It has been there all along because we have stored it there. At the needed moment, the correct moment, God called it to remembrance. But for Him to find it, it had to be there—a treasure hidden in our heart, an idea growing alone in a sheltered place. God gives us the joy of expression. Our words will have life because they have received the breath of God, causing them to live. This Word we proclaim is the living Word.

## Think on These Things

1. Compile a comprehensive bibliography for personal and professional enrichment. Correspond with seminary libraries to request book lists recommended by their faculties.
2. Examine titles on the current best-sellers lists. What trends in general reading interests do you discern?
3. Devise a plan for personal devotional reading of the Bible. Set specific goals and plan for their achievement in thirty-sixty-ninety-day increments.
4. Keep a journal of your readings during a week when you seek to expand your store of knowledge for sermon building. List ideas and insights which speak to you. What conclusions may you reach about which sources are most helpful?
5. Select from the following list a preacher in whose career you have interest. Study his biography to

determine how he cultivated the rich ideas that became his sermons.
   a. Charles Haddon Spurgeon
   b. G. Campbell Morgan
   c. Leslie D. Weatherhead
   d. Harry Emerson Fosdick
   e. George W. Truett
6. Explore the subject "The Holy Spirit in Preaching" through a careful examination of the Book of Acts.
7. List the ten areas of interest which you identify from conversations with your fellow church members. How many of these have become themes for sermons? Which have been ignored in preaching?

**Suggested Readings**

Bright, John. *The Authority of the Old Testament.* Nashville: Abingdon Press, 1967

Fisher, Fred L. *Prayer in the New Testament.* Philadelphia: The Westminster Press, 1964.

Fletcher, Jesse C. *Practical Discipleship.* Nashville: Broadman Press, 1980.

Hinson, E. Glenn. *Seekers After Mature Faith: A Historical Introduction to the Classics of Christian Devotion.* With special psychological commentary by Wayne Oates. Nashville: Broadman Press, 1968.

Lewis, C. S. *Surprised by Joy: The Shape of My Early Life.* New York: Harcourt, Brace & World, Inc., 1955.

Shannon, Harper. *Trumpets in the Morning.* Nashville: Broadman Press, 1969.

Shoemaker, Sam. *Extraordinary Living for Ordinary Men.* Grand Rapids: Zondervan Publishing House, 1965.

Thielicke, Helmut. *Our Heavenly Father: Sermons on the Lord's Prayer.* Trans. with an Introduction by John W. Doberstein. New York: Harper & Brothers, 1960.

### Notes

1. Merrill R. Abbey. *The Word Interprets Us* (New York: Agingdon Press, 1967).
2. We recommend devotional classics such as Thomas à Kempis, the *Imitation of Christ*. Also, Oswald Chambers published a series of booklets, among which *My Utmost for His Highest* and *The Love of God* are widely read.
3. Clyde Fant's "Noble Six–fold Path to Reading" informs this discussion. See *Preaching for Today*, pp. 131-32.
4. See the introduction by Ralph L. Lewis and Gregg Lewis, *Inductive Preaching: Helping People Listen* (Westchester, Ill.: Crossway Books, 1983), pp. 9-11.
5. Refer to Clowney, Daane, Fant, Lischer, and Rust in the suggested reading list and notes for chapter 1.
6. Recent one-volume theologies include: Dale Moody, *The Word of Truth.* (Grand Rapids: William B. Eerdmans Publishing Co., 1981); Hendrikus Berkhof, *Christian Faith: An Introduction to the Study of the Faith,* trans. Sierd Woudstra (Grand Rapids: William B. Eerdmans Publishing Company, 1978). One-volume Old and New Testament theologies by R. E. Clements, George Eldon Ladd, and Frank Stagg will be helpful.
7. See John 6:60-71, especially verse 68.

# 7
# The Structural Basis of Preaching

The structure of the sermon is the principal factor in recall of the sermon both for the minister and the congregation. Just as good interpretation leads to good preaching, good structure leads to clear, memorable preaching.

For some, the structure or organization of the sermon is a simple matter to decide. These preachers follow a basic two-, three-, or four-point development in every sermon. The only decision with regard to each text is how to make the text fit into the set structure. This is an indictment and for many the indictment applies. Our judgment grows out of listening to hundreds of sermons in classes and in churches. The majority of those sermons were three-point sermons, whatever the text. Preaching students, whose experience is limited, express surprise at the suggestion that sermons may be structured in other ways. Their reaction indicates that they, too, have determined that the three-point sermon is normative, if not obligatory, since that form has dominated their experience in hearing and preaching sermons. Our purpose is to present several possibilities for sermon structure and to affirm that the text should be

*The Structural Basis of Preaching*

a determining factor in selecting the appropriate organizational pattern for the message.[1]

## Bible Exposition as the Basis of Structure

All sermons should begin in biblical exposition. The sermons of the Old Testament prophets were repetitions of messages received directly from God. They were, in most cases, descriptions of God's actions or explanations of such subjects as repentance, judgment, or covenant obligations. The word of God came as a series of formal edicts, as in the case of the Decalogue, or as instructions for Israel to follow. After the Babylonian Exile, the prophets and priests began the custom of reading and commenting on the Scriptures. The practice of running commentary became known as a *homily*, from the Greek verb "to assemble," implying an assembly gathered to hear a speech or a sermon.

In the synagogue, the Service of the Word included the reading of selections from the Old Testament Scriptures, the Law and the Prophets. An explanation of the meaning of a passage read, a homily, followed. Occasionally a guest rabbi would be asked to read and comment (see Luke 4:16-21). The discussions were always based on the passage read. New Testament sermons conform somewhat to this pattern, especially Simon Peter's sermon on the day of Pentecost and Stephen's defense in Acts 6. The homily remains a popular sermon form today.

Through the influence of Greek and Roman rhetorical thought, preachers of the first three Christian centuries began to structure their sermons on bases other than a running commentary. They framed, as well, more unifying themes. According to E. C. Dargan, from approximately the end of the third century forward, the term *expository sermon* was applied *to a discourse with more orderly structure.*[2] A distinction between homily and expository sermons was made on the bases of theme and structure. An effort to simplify resulted in the differentiation between homily and expository sermons based on the number of verses employed in the text. Eventually, the practice of preaching on themes led to a third classification—the topical sermon. The result was the classification of sermons as textual (one or two verses of Scripture), expository (more than two verses), and topical (a biblical theme found in one or more passages).[3]

Our premise is that all sermons should first be expositions of Scripture. To determine what structure may serve best for a particular text, first consider the extent of the passage from which you will preach. What is the text? The answer to that question helps determine the approach to the sermon. We base our sermon structure upon our determination of the scope of the text and, more importantly, upon the message which speaks to us from it.

Interpretation and discovery of meaning lead to an understanding of the text. When exposition suggests the organizational pattern to be used in the development of the sermon, the following occurs:
1. The extent of the text is determined.
2. Exposition of the text follows:
    a. Reading and rereading the text from various translations and from Greek or Hebrew

*The Structural Basis of Preaching*

    b. Identifying pivotal meaning conveyed in specific components of the text: verses, phrases, words, quotations, or paraphrases of other scriptural truth
    c. Reviewing sources which deal with the text and with components identified as pivotal
    d. Reconstructing the broader context for the passage
    e. Identifying relevant historical perspectives
    f. Discovery of important personal considerations (identity, motivations, relationships of the writer or those who have a bearing on the passage—those addressed or described)
    g. Reaching a determination about the meaning of the passage, balancing untutored and tutored reactions to the passage

3. Identifying the means by which the truth of the text is best conveyed:
    a. Is the major thrust of the text summarized within the passage in a single verse or other identifiable unit of Scripture? If the answer is yes, the structure of the sermon should be based upon that limited portion, the text derived from exposition and interpretation; the remainder of the passage forms the Scripture lesson which may be read during the worship service when the sermon is to be preached.
    b. If the major thrust of the passage is not reducible to a core of insight summarized in a small unit of the text, but is found instead in the presentation of the broader passage as a whole, the preacher must then identify those salient concepts and

restate them as major units within the structure of the message he will present.
4. If the sermon structure is suggested by the limited core of understanding identified through 3.a, the message is a homily. If the sermon structure is suggested by the passage as a whole identified through 3.b, the message is an expository sermon.

For example, consider Romans 4, which speaks of Abraham's justification by faith. The entire chapter becomes the text since exposition reveals the necessity of considering the text as a whole. Now refer to John 3:1-15. In his interview with Nicodemus, Jesus declared: "Truly, truly, I say to you, unless one is born anew, he cannot see the kingdom of God" (v. 3). That one verse may become the basis of a sermon since the truth of it undergirds the entire story. In the first example, Romans 4, restatement of the entire chapter for the text will be normative; in the second, John 3:3, one verse will serve as the text and will be helped to speak for itself essentially as two points. Thus, sermon form may be based on the determination of how the text speaks best.

The preacher who develops the habit of studying Scripture will naturally begin to cultivate skill in discerning the shape of the text. The way it speaks to him probably will be the way it speaks best to his congregation.

### Biblical Literary Genre as the Basis of Structure

The exposition of the Scripture may lead the preacher to an awareness that the structure of his sermon will be determined by the literary form which clothes the truth. We consider the following sermon forms to be genre related: devotional sermons, narrative sermons, and didactic sermons.

**Devotional Sermons**

The text, Psalm 23, is devotional in nature. The mood of the passage is one of assurance, dependence, and confidence. From the first phrase the psalm draws the reader into the spirit of the writer, one who trusts in his Lord explicitly. The psalm seems to require a talk-through approach which will invite the listener to become involved with the psalmist in the depth of emotion which grows out of reflection upon the God who provides for his children in a manner similar to that of a shepherd providing for his flock. The preacher will present the units of thought as they occur and pause for consideration of each one. "The Lord is my shepherd" is an excellent idea which needs some time to impress itself upon the listener. "I shall not want" speaks of the shepherd's provision for all necessities. This kind of sermon is not concerned primarily with point structure. The psalmist appears to have been thinking aloud about the excellence of the care of God who is a shepherd to him.

A New Testament parallel to Psalm 23 appears in John 10 (especially vv. 11-18). Jesus identified Himself as a shepherd, fulfillment of the image expressed by the Old Testament psalmist. The form of John 10 compares favorably with Psalm 23. A sermon on the passage may follow the same structure, a commentary on Christ as the Lord, the shepherd of loving care for the believer.

Devotional structure follows the organizational pattern of the passage of Scripture upon which it is based.

Since its language is highly imagistic, it would be a mistake not to consider carefully the exposition step in preparing the message. The spirit of a devotional message is contemplative. The purpose of the sermon normally is to stimulate. Generally, devotional messages extol the characteristics of God to whom all devotion is given.

**Narrative Sermons**

Much of the Bible is narrative. The story of Adam and Eve is a dramatic account of how humankind was placed in the creation of the world. Contained in their story is every person's story. A sermon on humanity could assume the form of a retelling of the event from God's creation of man and woman through the expulsion of Adam and Eve from the Garden of Eden. At the conclusion of the narrative, the preacher could speak of the great truths revealed in their story: God's intent for human beings, humanity's freedom of choice, the entrance of sin into the history of the world, and the effects of sin.

Obviously we could develop topical messages on these concepts. And yet, narrative material in the Scriptures speaks best in that form. Typically we have looked for lessons contained in the Bible stories, ferreted them out, enumerated them, and provided our own illustrations to make their meaning clear. But stories as stories carry and reveal truths which become evident as they unfold. Why not recount the biblical narratives and allow the Spirit to make clear the truths contained as the listener follows the development of the stories?

*The Structural Basis of Preaching* **155**

Narrative preaching is one of the surest ways to recapture biblical theology in the form in which it first was delivered to us.[4] The Bible was initially a story told. The first Christian preaching was a telling and retelling of the story of Jesus reaching its climax in the resurrection.[5] The recent interest in narrative preaching has encouraged renewed emphasis upon sound biblical preaching.

Narratives abound in the Bible, particularly in the Old Testament. Sermons which retell the narratives will fall on ears which recognize their content. The call and life story of Abraham and all the patriarchs are familiar to most believers. The Book of Exodus is a picture of God's redemption of humankind from the bondage of sin. A narrative thread unites the diverse literature of the Old Testament.

The life and ministry of Jesus Christ in the New Testament is the story of God's coming to humankind. Although the separate accounts in the Gospels do not form a complete biography of the Savior, the resources are rich which describe God's dramatic intervention in human history to reveal Himself. The narrative of the church on mission speaks eloquently to an imperative to witness which we share with our spiritual ancestors.

Some approaches to narrative go beyond the telling of the biblical narrative. For example, the preacher may retell a biblical story by relating the same truth with contemporary characters, setting, and language. The dramatic nature of Saul's conversion has recurred in the salvation of persons in every generation. To tell their stories is to tell Saul's story.

Also, the story of the impulsive prodigal and the love of his patient father is repeated often. A seminary student told about a young man who denounced his upbringing, his parents, and his hometown, and then left home, embittered and angry. For years his family did not hear from him or see him. Then, one day, he returned and asked his parents to let him move back into their home. He was bereft of friends and funds. His health and spirit were broken. His parents gladly received him and never referred to his running away. Then the student revealed that he was that runaway son. The prodigal lived again through his testimony, as did the waiting father.

In addition, the presentation of a biblical character in a costumed, dramatic monologue may be a narrative sermon. The minister may cast himself in the role of Joseph, Samson, Gideon, David, Peter, or Paul and recite an event from the life of the personality directly from Scripture or retell it in his own words. The preacher will require extensive preparation and genuine skill if he chooses to identify fully with a Bible person in this way.

Another possibility exists in making narrative a vehicle through which a nonnarrative text may speak. This approach requires a plot, characters, development of a theme, and a climax or conclusion.[6] Numerous Scripture passages have all of these in the background. Knowledge of Bible history, coupled with imagination and creativity, enables the preacher to construct a narrative through which the text may speak. Paul's closing remarks about his life (2 Tim. 4:6-8) provide an excellent basis upon which to preach such a sermon.

## Didactic Sermons

Much of the biblical material is didactic or instructional in nature. The Sermon on the Mount is a primary example. Jesus preached in a series of epigrammatic statements. Numerous comparisons with the Proverbs may be made as well as with the Old Testament books of Law (teachings).

In order to find a sermon form suitable to convey the lessons of the Sermon on the Mount, the preacher should outline the Sermon and identify the individual points made by Jesus. Consider Matthew 5:1-13, generally known as the Beatitudes. Each is a singular statement of fact. It follows that a good way to preach on each is to make each Beatitude into a one-point sermon, in the form of a declaration made, explained, supported with proof and illustrations, and applied. No straining at structure can result in a better form than the one in which the Beatitudes appear.

Later in the Sermon, the nature of the material provides the preacher an excellent opportunity for comparison-contrast sermon forms. "You have heard . . . but I say unto you . . ." is the pattern (Matt. 5:21 *ff.*). The natural plan of development would be to restate the Old Testament passage to which Christ referred and tell its meaning. Then, return to Jesus' teaching to reveal how He brought the Old Testament lesson to fulfillment (Matt. 5:17). This particular form of sermon is figuratively a way of holding up two photographs and describing how the second teaches the same lesson as the first, but to a much greater degree of completeness.

Beyond the Gospels, the New Testament contains a wealth of didactic material. The three Epistles of John provide examples of love in action. The Book of Hebrews clarifies much of the teaching about priesthood in didactic form. Paul's instructions to the young Timothy came in the form of reminders of lessons previously learned.

**Other Genre-Related Sermons**

Other kinds of literature appear in the Bible, among them poetry, complete with parallelism, rhythm, progress or movement, and comparison of thought. Much work remains to be done on elements of Hebrew poetry as suggestive of sermon form. Biography is a significant part of biblical literature. For example, the narrative of the patriarchs (Gen. 12—50) suggests a number of character sermons. Such sermons could build on descriptions of qualities found in Bible personalities, with a call for similar qualities to become part of the present day servants of God. Major personalities include Abraham, Issac, Jacob, Sarah, Rebecca, and Joseph. Others in the accounts also are worthy of consideration. Eleazar, Laban, Leah, Esau, and Reuben all play somewhat lesser roles but are, nevertheless, important to the completion of the drama. Genesis 28—50 contains a fine biography of Joseph.

The biographical sermon may be very effective. People are interested in one another. Human interest increases dramatically when the sermon paints a personality portrait. Identifying with Bible persons, the listener may find application in the sermon naturally, on his own.

# The Structural Basis of Preaching

Some Bible personalities stand out who are not just part of a larger narrative. Paul, for example, named Demas as one of his followers who left the work of ministry because of his love for the world. Phoebe, the deaconness, stands out. Stephen, one of the first deacons, provides the preacher with a study in service and martyrdom. A sermon on Stephen could follow the list of qualifications given for the first seven set aside to help the apostles with the business of the church. Philip, another of the deacons, serves as an example for following the Spirit's leadership in evangelism.

## Topical Bases of Structure

Some specific passages of Scripture suggest sermon ideas and set the preacher to looking for ways to express them. On the other hand, some topics or subjects demand attention in a comprehensive preaching plan; the preacher looks for selected passages with which to support the development of certain aspects of the topics. Topical bases of structure are employed for doctrinal, problem-solution, life-situation, and confessional sermons.

### The Doctrinal Sermon

Topics frequently employ multiple passage texts and, as a consequence, a more formalized point structure for the sermon. If you decide to develop a sermon on the doctrine of salvation, you will likely construct the sermon as a topical message. Throughout the New Testament there are abundant texts on salvation. The preacher may wish to develop a three-point sermon on the steps to salvation employing Romans 3:23; 6:23; and

5:8 as his points. That would give him a simply structured, multipassage, topical sermon. Other great doctrines, such as the church, the priesthood of the believer, eschatology, and the Holy Spirit, lend themselves to similar development.

The sermon on doctrine may grow out of a single text as well. John 3:16 is a self-contained passage full of truth about salvation. The words of Jesus in Matthew 16:18 provide ample content for a sermon on the church. In John 16:7-16, Jesus stated at least three remarkable truths about the work of the Holy Spirit.

Varied forms of biblical literature can be employed to teach doctrine. Consider Matthew 25:1-13, the parable of the wise and foolish virgins, as an example of the need for preparation for the return of Christ. Matthew 13 contains a series of parables which speak directly about the nature of the kingdom of heaven (these are didactic in nature, with much doctrinal value). In all these cases, the topic determines the selection of the text; in turn, the text may determine the shape of the sermon. Yet, the meaning of the text is never minimized or ignored. The topic should never violate the meaning of the text.

### The Life-Situation Sermon

Selection of the text (or texts) on the basis of the topic is nowhere more evident than in the life-situation sermon. The idea for such a sermon generally comes from the preacher's knowledge of life gained through observation, pastoral contacts, or general cultural awareness.

Observers of the human condition will encounter signs of loneliness, despair, anger, sorrow, failure, doubt, worry, stress—the list appears endless. Pastors feel a special need to bring a word from God to address the crises of life. Once again, the topic arises first in his mind and sends him to the Bible to find a relevant passage for speaking on the subject. While the topic may determine structure, the text determines content.

Let us look at the subject of worry as an example of a life-situation sermon. One of the major concerns for the person who worries is: How am I going to handle my worry? The preacher responds, naturally: "Depend on God. Turn your worries over to him." Immediately thereafter the preacher seeks biblical support for his approach. He does not have to look far. Matthew 6:25-34 contains an elaborate statement on how to handle worry. It speaks of reliance on God who cares for all his creation, especially people. Christ says it in almost the same words: "Do not worry. Trust your Heavenly Father to take care of you" (authors' translation).

Another life situation which all humans encounter sooner or later is grief. Generally death creates our need to cope with grief, though there are other causes. How can we handle our grief? Counselors tell us to face up to it honestly, admit its effect on us, and work through the deep-as-life struggle to the point of control. Having expressed his conviction about grief, again the minister turns to the Bible for validation of his approach. There is good material in the reaction of David to the death of his rebellious son, Absalom (2 Sam. 13:1 to 19:8, especially 18:24 to 19:8). David wept bitterly at the news of his son's death, though the boy had brought much sorrow to him. David openly grieved but in time found control through the restoration of balance in his experience. God's comfort became real to him.

## The Problem-Solution Sermon

The distinction between a life-situation sermon and a problem-solution sermon is a slight one. The first is more therapeutic in nature; the second is more ethical. The need for problem-solution preaching often comes from moral and ethical issues which demand immediate resolution, issues which will not always allow for the passage of time and working through to a satisfactory conclusion.

A young person may confront such a crisis with the first temptation to drink or to take drugs. If the youth has been prepared to deal with the problem, he or she may resolve the crisis with a firm refusal. The local pastor senses the need to prepare youth and others through sermons on how to handle temptation and on the proper care of one's body. His instructions will need behind them all the weight and authority of Scripture.

Temptation is common to us all. It came even to Christ. His experience with the tempter in Matthew 4:1-14 (compare Luke 4:1-14) is filled with the correct responses in the face of temptation. Concern for proper care of the body is the subject of 1 Corinthians 3:16 and 6:16, Paul's admonition to remember that the body is the temple of the Holy Spirit. Paul himself constantly kept his body under subjection, knowing its importance to him in the service of Christ his Lord.

Again, in the problem-solution sermon, the subject occurs first to the preacher as he confronts a moral or ethical dilemma (as a result of observation of his people or of society about him). He has deep convictions about the solution, which grow out of his knowledge of

## The Structural Basis of Preaching

Scripture and his personal commitment to right and goodness. He marshals the Scriptures in support of those convictions. The arrangement of the sermon grows from his careful study of the topic informed by the texts, correctly understood, to give the sermon biblical authority. The minister's opinion, if not supported by the text, is subject to the same judgment as anyone else's opinion. He may be wrong. Yet, with the authority of the Bible, he may be confident in his proclamation.

Topics which may be classified as problem-solution include alcohol and drug abuse, abortion, euthanasia, voting for particular issues or candidates, and other questions which may arise instantaneously and must be resolved immediately. These continue to surface in a highly permissive culture. In a majority of these cases, the preacher must do his preaching before the problem has run its course. He should strive to establish principles by which such decisions readily can be made when the need arises. The preacher will perceive that ethical and moral issues recur. He will feel compelled to assert biblical solutions which the Christian community can implement. It may be disappointing or discouraging that the solutions must be offered over and over. The problem-solution sermon will not solve moral and ethical issues once and for all. The preacher, however, must *keep on solving the problems* in the conviction that each effort moves the Christian closer to a final resolution of the problem area.

**The Confessional Sermon**

John Claypool, in his Lyman Beecher Lectures of 1979,[7] acquaints us with a style of sermon called confessional preaching. The confessional sermon is one in which the preacher discusses openly and frankly his own struggles with difficulty and reveals, usually at the conclusion of the sermon, how he handled the hardship by relying on faith to sustain him.

Claypool's model provides instruction for responding to death and dying, physical handicaps, divorce, and doubts. The distinction of confessional preaching compared with the two previous kinds of sermons is slight but discernible. Only a minister confident in his grounding in faith can make a full disclosure of such a personal nature.[8]

The structure of a confessional sermon will follow the development of the struggle. Points may correspond with stages of life, changes in attitude, and small victories won. A full narrative of the events may provide the most suitable form for the sermon. One or more biblical principles may provide the scriptural support. On the other hand, the entire contents of the faith may be the point of reference. In either case, the Bible is the authority.

## Intended Response as the Basis of Structure

Earlier we suggested four basic purposes in preaching—to inform, stimulate, convince, and persuade. With each sermon, one also will formulate a specific objective which is the action or response called for in the sermon. The intended response may be a determinant in the shaping of the sermon structure.

First, consider the sermon based on the intended response to inform. The doctrinal sermon or the didactic sermon may be preached in order to inform the listeners.

## The Structural Basis of Preaching

The purpose may prompt the preacher to structure his points in the following manner: the progression from the easiest facts to understand to the most difficult. For a sermon on the doctrine of creation, the text may come from Genesis 1—3. The days of creation or the order in which the earth and its inhabitants were created would preserve the integrity of the text and provide a lucid framework for the message.

Another sermon to inform, a study of the biblical instruction on relationships within the home, could be based on passages found in Ephesians 5:22 to 6:4, 1 Peter 3:10-17, or Colossians 3. For his structure, the preacher may follow the pattern of Paul in Ephesians 5:22 to 6:4. First, he pinpointed the responsibility of the wife to the husband. Next, he addressed the necessity for the husband to love the wife. They, together, submit to one another in the fear of the Lord. Then, Paul instructed the children about their behavior toward parents. He closed with words about parental discipline and instruction.

In both instances, the preacher's intent determines his structure. He must have a biblical foundation upon which to build his sermon. Other models from the Scriptures are instructive: The sermon to inform may be a short story, a parable with a lesson contained in it. It may be an object lesson: Jesus held up a coin when he wanted to teach a lesson on paying tribute. Furthermore, it may be a listing of traits to be desired in a Christan's life, perhaps using a Bible person as a reference point, with the intent not only to list the traits but also to inform the listeners that they can acquire or develop them. An appropriate test for this kind of preaching is to ask the question: How can I best pass along information to my hearers? A model for teaching will become a model for preaching.

Second, the sermon based on the purpose to stimulate seeks to rekindle the faith of the believer in order to help her regain its vitality and energy. This will often be an appeal to memory: The recalling of one's initial fervor in the service of the Lord should stir a member to renewal of commitment and lead her into new areas of service or the resumption of old ones.

Another sermon might assume the form of a challenge in order to stimulate the listeners. Preachers sometimes fail to be bold enough in the proclamation of the Word. Elijah's confrontation with the prophets of Baal on Mount Carmel came in the form of a challenge. He sought to renew the allegiance of Israel to the one true God. Joshua challenged all the Israelite households to serve God and declared his own intention to serve along with his household. His purpose was to stimulate the devotion of Israel to God's law.

In a similar way, the preacher may stimulate by stressing the results of certain courses of action. Jesus told the seventy to go and preach (Luke 10:1-20). He cautioned them that, in some cities, persons would refuse them but that the disciples were to persevere; they were helping to bring in the kingdom. Upon the completion of their mission, the seventy returned to Jesus, rejoicing that even the devils were subject to them through His name. He told the seventy to rejoice more because their names were written in heaven.

The sermon to stimulate or revive builds upon commitment made in past time. The hearer is not necessarily confronted with new ideas or unfamiliar

*The Structural Basis of Preaching*

concepts from Scripture. This objective recognizes that at times Christian devotion diminishes in force. A sermon designed to stimulate will recall such a person to loyalty in the ministry of the church and to greater contentment and victory in daily life.

Third, the sermon to convince strives to gain agreement. The doctrinal sermon and a sermon on resolution of conflict or forgiveness are examples. In a doctrinal sermon, the specific objective is to convince Christians of the correctness of a teaching of the church. Sermon form may be determined by the sequence in which the biblical teaching occurs. As a responsible interpreter of Scripture, the preacher uses a systematic approach to a particular doctrine. His intention is not to convince his listeners merely to agree with him: He must seek to present biblical doctrine as it is found in Scriptures.

The sermon to convince relies on the presentation of sound evidence drawn from biblical and extrabiblical material. Form may follow a particular line of reasoning which naturally will lead to the acceptance of the sermon's affirmation. Another possibility for sermon form is a series of affirmations to which the listener is asked to give consent. If the listener accepts the statements one at a time, he must accept the sum of which each is a part. A sermon on eschatology may be presented in this manner.

    I. Christ said He would return to the earth.
   II. The angels echoed the promises that Christ would come again.
  III. The apostles reiterated the promise.
  IV. Thus, Christ is coming again.

Usually, a sermon on this topic emphasizes the fulfillment of signs of end times as perceived by the preacher. Remember, however, that our purpose is not to present our view on the subject and convince the listeners to agree with it!

As with other sermon forms, the preacher carefully relies on the support of extrabiblical material in his presentation. He will want to remember that no illustration from such sources should contradict or belie his biblical material. He must not, on the other hand, rearrange biblical material in a manner that would cause it to appear to prove something which it does not or in a way that would cause the Bible to speak against itself. Synthetic order, rearrangement of textual materials, treads close to manipulation. Always allow the Bible to speak for itself.

Fourth, the sermon to persuade includes our preaching directed toward hearer action. When our sermons are persuasive, our objective is for our listeners to do something. Of course, the response is left to the hearers and the counsel of the Holy Spirit which they follow. But the role of the preacher is to present the sermon as persuasively as he can to make a compelling case for the right course of action. The force of the Word of God will be the principal means through which an individual will discern the course of action to follow. The preacher will wish, however, to present the claim of the text and his message in such a way that response will be a natural conclusion to the hearing of the Word.

The evangelistic sermon is a basic example of the sermon to persuade. It may not be so much a logical presentation to lead to a decision as it may be a testimony

## The Structural Basis of Preaching

from Scripture with which we reason about the need for and the worth of salvation.

Testimony from Scripture presents living evidence of the reality of salvation. It can be corroborated easily from the lives and testimonies of contemporary Christians. The sermon may be fashioned along the lines of the sinner's progression to the point of salvation. Awareness of sin, repentance, confession, belief (or faith), and baptism are the "steps" of the progression. A very effective way to preach an evangelistic sermon is to tell the story of the convert and point to the "steps" of conversion as they appear in the story. That provides an attractive variation of the first-, second-, and third-point approach.

The Bible contains an abundance of salvation testimonies, ranging from the dramatic turnabout by Saul on the road to Damascus to Matthew's quiet response to the Savior's invitation to follow Him.

Moreover, there are other passages which instruct the nonbeliever in the way of belief. The Philippian jailer was told to believe (Acts 16:31); Nicodemus was instructed to be born again (John 3:1 *ff.*); Jesus stated that to come through Him is the only way to the Father (John 14:6; 6:60 *ff.*).

The practice of Jesus and the apostles was to point the way and invite the hearer to follow. In their practice lies the foundation upon which the modern invitation is built.[9] The contemporary evangelistic sermon generally concludes with an appeal to accept God's terms for salvation.

Comparison and contrast is an effective method for preaching an evangelistic sermon. Ephesians 2:1-10, for example, presents the "then" of the sinner as death and the "now" of the believer as "life." Salvation as resurrection from the dead is a striking proclamation and is a restatement of the original *kerygma* of resurrection Sunday. Paul's Epistles contain numerous comparisons: darkness and light, aliens and citizens, and strangers and fellow saints. The sermon form may present the "before" and the "after" pictures of salvation.

In addition to evangelistic themes, the sermons designed to motivate action in stewardship, mission support, witness, social action, or volunteer service in the educational or other ministries of the church may require persuasive development. The preacher may find the stock issues of a proposition of policy helpful as he develops persuasive strategies: the statement of *need*, proposal of a *plan* to meet the need, and description of the *benefits* which will follow the implementation of the plan. A call to action concludes the persuasive appeal.

## Beginning, Middle, End

Regardless of the kind of structure employed, every sermon should begin, progress, and end well. The principles suggested in this section will apply to every form.

No part of the sermon is more important than the beginning. If he begins well, the preacher will usually continue well. The reverse of that dictum also holds true. In the first minute or two of the sermon, the preacher seeks to introduce his idea and get the listeners involved in that idea.

The preacher has two choices in the introduction: he may begin with the contemporary moment and move to

## The Structural Basis of Preaching

the text (inductive beginning), or he may begin with the text and bring the idea to the contemporary moment (deductive beginning). In the inductive approach, begin with a quotation from a newspaper, a statistic, a striking sentence, a question, or a short illustration. The deductive introduction generally begins with an explanation of the text, restatement of the text, or a narrative from the Bible. The inductive approach is stated in the present tense; the deductive in the past tense.

There are advantages and disadvantages in each type of introduction. With the inductive style, the most obvious advantage is that the hearer feels involved in the sermon because of material addressed directly to him in the present tense, *or* he hears about the world in which we live. The clearest disadvantage is that the preacher has an obligation to find an acceptable way of taking the listener to the world and meaning of the text. He must bridge from his world to the ancient world of the Bible.

In the deductive introduction, the primary advantage for the preacher is that he immediately is identified with biblical material and the assumption that biblical exposition is the basis of the sermon. The singular disadvantage of the deductive beginning is that the preacher will have to find an acceptable way to bring the past into the present, to bridge from the world in the past to the present. To be sure, the biblical material has, in itself, a quality of timelessness which the Spirit makes known to the individual listener. Yet, the preacher bears the responsibility of clear and relevant application so the hearer can see the timely in the timeless truths the preacher presents.

Other sermon forms have beginnings which stem

from the nature of the developmental pattern. The narrative sermon, for example, begins simply with the story. Jesus provided a clear model with his parable of the prodigal: "A certain man had two sons . . ."(Luke 15:11, KJV). "The Lord is my light, and my salvation" (Ps. 27:1) provides a good, striking sentence of affirmation for a devotional sermon on God's care for His children.

The sermon introduction will gain attention, state or imply the affirmation. It will provide a preliminary indication for the movement of the message, set essential background information, define terms, or offer required explanations. It will also foster natural advancement into the body of the message.

Sermons should have progression and movement. After the beginning elements are in place, the preacher should move on to the middle portion of the sermon, the body of the message. Unless the structure is a narrative, you will facilitate movement and achieve unity with the use of transition sentences. The transition may come in the form of a question, a restatement of the affirmation, or with a "therefore" kind of statement (for which we have ample biblical precedent in the writing of Paul).

With the narrative sermon form, the plot development moves the story toward its climax.[10] The preacher who preaches narrative sermons will develop a sense for the movement of the sermon and will retell it, naturally, as he feels it. The middle portion of the sermon will be the revelation of the central thought or character trait upon which the narrative depends. To return to the story of the prodigal, the story turns on the son's realization that he had come to the end of his resources and the remembrance of his father's house.

## The Structural Basis of Preaching

The middle of the sermon with divisions of the subject or points for structure contains those points and their development. Not only should there be a transition from the introduction to the body of the message but the sermon also should contain smooth transitions from point to point within the middle *and* from it to the conclusion. Here the preacher's concern should be with unity, clarity, progression, and orderly movement. Each point needs to be a division of the subject or affirmation. If there is division, no fewer than two points are possible. Subdivision of each point requires a minimum of two subpoints. Division beyond two subpoints can contribute to confusion. Moreover, minute subdivision hampers clarity, unity, and brevity.

We explain and illustrate our major divisions and subdivisions. One can easily see how a sermon will be longer as we seek to develop more points. Total time involved in the sermon presentation is a factor to be considered with each sermon, especially if the sermons are part of a broadcast.

The conclusion of the sermon is equal to the introduction in importance. Simply stated, the conclusion should successfully bring the sermon to an end. To move from the body to the conclusion, you should have a transitional sentence. "This, then, is the plan . . ." may provide the transition. "As a result of these actions, we learn . . ." is another possible way to direct attention toward the conclusion.

Having shifted the attention toward the conclusion, move on to the end. Never promise "Finally," only to go on with no intention to stop. Successful ways to end the sermon include summary of the main divisions of the subject, restatement of the affirmation accompanied by reference to the sermon's progression, statement of the obvious conclusion to be reached, and an illustration of the central truth the sermon explored. The conclusion is the last opportunity you have to make application.

A clue to the nature of your conclusion can be gained by reviewing the intent and specific objective of the sermon. Include your purpose in the conclusion, and it will provide an effective transition into the invitation. Let the conclusion get to the main point of the entire sermon and clarify, again, the purpose for which you preached the sermon.

The narrative sermon also contains its own conclusion, in the form of the climax or moment of highest interest. The ending of the sermon may be signaled through the creation of that climactic moment. The prodigal came to himself, returned to his father, and learned that his father was waiting for him to come home. That is the high point of the story; it speaks for itself.

Often in a narrative sermon, the preacher will tell the biblical story, or retell it in contemporary terms, and then state the lessons for his listeners which grow out of the narrative. In that case, he concludes the story and makes application based upon the entire story. He may also allow the conclusion of the story to be the lesson of the entire sermon. In both approaches he retains the conclusion of the narrative and facilitates application directly or indirectly.

## Organize for Inclusion and Recall

The preacher who carefully organizes his thoughts and places them in a structured way in his sermons will gain the advantage of being inclusive: He will analyze the message, note lapses and voids in his presentation, and counter them through thorough preparation. He will have a blueprint for his sermon which will afford a view of its proportion and balance. He can perceive strengths and weaknesses. The blueprint may be carried into the pulpit as outline or notes or the structure may be committed to memory to facilitate preaching without notes. The help to recall which benefits the preacher will benefit the hearer as well. A well-organized, carefully structured message can be retained in the memory of the hearer and provide the impetus needed for believing or doing what the sermon affirms.

### Think on These Things

1. Read and analyze three contemporary examples of the homily. On the basis of your study, formulate a definition of this sermon form.
2. Survey a comprehensive anthology of preaching to discern the extent of doctrinal preaching. Upon what doctrinal issues are sermons based most frequently?
3. Explore advantages and disadvantages of life-situation preaching. Problem-solution preaching.
4. Develop the concept: "Biblical exposition is the basis of all preaching."
5. Construct a bibliography of genre-related sermons. Upon which literary forms are sermons most often developed? Which forms seem neglected?
6. Write an introduction to a sermon consciously employing the principles discussed in this chapter.

7. Find five examples of attention-getting titles for sermons. Why are they attention arresting? Do they in all cases represent faithfully the content of the sermons?
8. Outline approaches to message conclusion. What ought to be avoided in concluding a sermon?
9. How may one bridge from message to invitation to response?
10. Examine the sermons of one contemporary preacher focusing upon the use of illustrations. Analyze their aptness and the skill the preacher employs as he works them into the continuity of the sermon.

## Suggested Readings

Best, Ernest. *From Text to Sermon: Responsible Use of the New Testament in Preaching.* Atlanta: John Knox Press, 1978.

Craddock, Fred B. *As One Without Authority.* 3rd edition. Nashville: Abingdon, 1979.

_____. *Overhearing the Gospel.* Nashville: Abingdon, 1978.

Davis, Henry Grady. *Design for Preaching.* Philadelphia: Muhlenberg Press, 1958.

Jensen, Richard A. *Telling the Story: Variety and Imagination in Preaching.* Minneapolis: Augsburg Publishing House, 1980.

Keck, Leander E. *The Bible in the Pulpit: The Renewal of Biblical Preaching.* Nashville: Abingdon, 1978.

Kaiser, Walter C., Jr. *The Old Testament in Contemporary Preaching.* Ontario Bible College, The Elmore Harris Series, No. 3. Grand Rapids: Baker Book House, 1973.

Massey, James Earl. *Designing the Sermon: Order and Movement in Preaching.* Abingdon Preacher's Library, edited by William D. Thompson. Nashville: Abingdon, 1980.

Skinner, Craig. *The Teaching Ministry of the Pulpit: Its History, Theology, Psychology, and Practice for Today.* Grand Rapids: Baker Book House, 1973.

Steimle, Edmund A.; Niedenthal, Morris J.; and Rice, Charles L. *Preaching the Story.* Philadelphia: Fortress Press, 1980.

Stroup, George W. *The Promise of Narrative Theology: Recovering the Gospel in the Church.* Atlanta: John Knox Press, 1981.

Taylor, Gardner C. *How Shall They Preach?* Elgin, Illinois: Progressive Baptist Publishing House, 1977.

### Notes

1. Compare Don M. Wardlaw, ed., *Preaching Biblically: Creating Sermons in the Shape of Scripture* (Philadelphia: Westminster Press, 1983), pp. 15; 18-23.
2. Edwin C. Dargan, *A History of Preaching*, Introduction by J. B. Weatherspoon (New York: George H. Doran Co., 1905; reprint ed., Grand Rapids: Baker Book House, 1968), 1, p. 41.
3. Andrew W. Blackwood, *Preaching from the Bible* (Nashville: Abingdon, 1941; reprint ed., Grand Rapids: Baker Book House, 1974), pp. 36-42.
4. George W. Stroup, *The Promise of Narrative Theology: Recovering the Gospel in the Church* (Atlanta: John Knox Press, 1981), pp. 70-97, especially p. 97.
5. Read the sermons of Simon Peter and Paul in the Book of Acts, especially 2:14-36; 13:14-41.
6. Compare Eugene L. Lowry, *The Homiletical Plot: The Sermon as Narrative Art Form* (Atlanta: John Knox Press, 1980), pp. 8-25.
7. John Claypool, *The Preaching Event*, Lyman Beecher Lectures, Yale University (Waco, Texas: Word Books, Publisher, 1980).
8. Some of the sermons of Harry Emerson Fosdick seem to fit this classification. See his *Riverside Sermons*, Introduction by Henry Pitney Van Dusen (New York: Harper & Brothers, Publishers, 1958), especially pp. 247-54.
9. Faris D. Whitesell, *Sixty-Five Ways to Give Evangelistic Invitations*, 3rd ed. (Grand Rapids: Zondervan Publishing House, 1945), pp. 11-16.
10. Lowry, p. 25.

# 8
## The Expressive Basis of Preaching

Preaching is a verbal art. The preacher speaks words carefully crafted to convey meaning. We define the expressive basis of preaching to include the choice of words and their combination into sentences, paragraphs, and longer units of discourse. The style of the preacher will inevitably reveal characteristic ways of expression which we identify as his "style." Vocabulary, idiomatic expressions, pet phrases, and even grammatical constructions afford clues to the nature of the preacher's style, his characteristic mode of expression.

Preaching is an oral medium of expression. We may study *sermons* from the distant past through manuscripts of messages preserved in written form. However, when we study *preaching* in the nineteenth century, for example, a complete reconstruction of the communicative event surrounding a sermon is impossible. We gather all the information we can about the setting, the audience, the message, and its presentation to describe the preaching of, say, Charles Haddon Spurgeon. While the reports of eyewitnesses are invaluable, we know our representation of Spurgeon's preaching to be at best partial.

## The Expressive Basis of Preaching

While we shall leave behind more extensive records of our preaching, students in the twenty-first century who look back to discern the nature of religious communication in the last quarter of our century will face a dilemma similar to ours: The sermon may be studied, but the total communicative situation cannot be definitively reproduced. The interaction of preacher and people in the presentation of the message is too complex: Inferences or educated guesses will be required to augment our technology.

Thus, the expressive basis of preaching focuses upon the words of spoken discourse: the language of preaching not the language of the sermon. The language of preaching exists momentarily as sound waves interpreted by the ear as separate, distinguishable elements of communication that must be immediately comprehended as words, phrases, sentences, and longer units of discourse which *mean something*. When the meaning derived from the words heard corresponds with the meaning intended by the preacher, the message is *clear*. When the language heard brings unconscious pleasure to the hearer by its aptness, its striking use of figurative expression, or its cogency, the message has *beauty*. For preaching to be clear and to possess beauty is a worthy goal for one charged with retelling the "old, old story of Jesus and his love." The writer of this gospel song may be close to the necessary prerequisite to clarity and beauty in the testimony: "I love to tell the story. . . ." Indeed, such motivation is essential to the toil required to achieve clearness and beauty in preaching. Good style requires hard work.

## Meaning and Language

Earlier we discussed the theology of preaching. We affirmed the Spirit's role in enlivening the message we proclaim. The words we speak communicate meaning at various levels. Our response to preaching depends upon the degree of theological maturity we have attained. Or, the apprehension of theological insights fosters the comprehension of meaning inherent in preaching. As we grow in spiritual maturity, expression of the faith should mean more to us.

If you have struggled with a "Children's Sermon," you know that a simple retelling of a biblical narrative or an explanation of a principle of the faith can be exceedingly difficult when it is to be shared with children from ages four to eleven. One such sermon based upon a portion of John 14:6, "Jesus said to him, 'I am the way. . . .,'" employed a simple narrative of two boys who take a bike ride to show a stranger the way to the nursing home nearby. The preacher then said, "Jesus' way is paved with unselfishness, love, truth, service, and sacrifice. He even gave his life so that others who followed after him would know that he was right." The narrative, although suited more to a small town than an urban setting, would be understood by preteen age bike riders. The teaching about Jesus, however, ignores the child's inclination to understand literally. The way paved with unselfishness would be lost upon a young child. The abstractions following would be but dimly perceived, if at all. The effort to explain Christ's death falls far short of an acceptable theological statement because the preacher in consideration of the age and

## The Expressive Basis of Preaching

experiences of his hearers has oversimplified a pivotal event in salvation history. Theological maturity brought to bear upon the metaphor means more than "I *show you* the way."

The development of skill with language proceeds from "what does this mean?" to "how does this mean?" as we become more aware of the complex nature of both language and meaning. The child is literal minded.[1] Symbolism and symbolic language and action are beyond him. High-level abstractions are often removed far from the child's everyday world. Their inclusion in teaching or conversation with children requires reduction of the abstraction to specific instances or examples within the experiences of the children. By grasping the example, the child will move toward the more sophisticated statement of a principle in the abstract concept.

We assimilate the conventions of language by a slow and unconscious process. The child is born into a language environment. Parents, grandparents, and others talk to a child from birth. There is no delay until the child can respond in kind. Such delay would merely postpone development of the means for response. Meantime, the child jabbers away forming the sounds he can make, discarding those he does not hear, retaining those he hears, those which occasion response when employed singly or in combination. An early, accidental "da-da" or "ma-ma" receives overwhelming reinforcement and a rudimentary understanding of *language* as *name* emerges in the consciousness of the child.

A child recreates the early Adamic task, "So out of the ground the Lord God formed every beast of the field and every bird of the air, and brought them to the man to see what he would call them; and whatever the man called every living creature, that was its name" (Gen. 2:19). Occasionally the child will rename an object. Her family may accept the new name. For a time the new designation will stand. When the child encounters its lack of acceptance in the broader community, it will be discarded.

A child comprehends his identity as embodied in the name given. A child may ask, "How did you know I was David and not some other little boy?" That question is in touch with a Hebrew understanding pervasive in the Scriptures of the Old and New Testament: Authority, identity, and action are embodied in the name. Harm done to the name is done to the person. Jacob became Israel; Simon became Cephas to mark a new purpose, to enhance a new identity.

The fact that revelation is verbal makes the discovery of the what and how of meaning almost as imperative as comprehending the who of meaning: Moses expected the children of Israel to ask who? how? and what? in that order. "The God of your fathers" identified as "I am who I am," "Yahweh," the Lord, the God of Abraham, the God of Isaac, and the God of Jacob is the "who" Moses required.

Indeed, God as *person* who *reveals* in *language* is the basic understanding essential to faith. God is not limited to language for revelation, but he has chosen language as the vehicle for its expression.[2] While he may speak in the whirlwind or the still, small voice, what he speaks becomes language at once, symbolic initially or following symbolic action. God speaks. Man responds in obedience or disobedience. The whole is told and set down in language for successive generations to experience.

Thus, at a rudimentary level, children employ the symbolic nature of language although comprehension of the essence of language as symbol remains obscure until facility with language becomes much more advanced. Gradually we disassociate name with identity; word with thing; symbol with reality. Gradually we expand our vocabularies and include more and more high-level abstractions which we may employ with meaning consistent with the understanding of others.

The preacher who stands in the verbal tradition of the God of Abraham, the God of Isaac, the God of Jacob, the God and Father of our Lord Jesus Christ, must use language well in his representation of the *who* of revelation, the *what*, and the *how*. He must recognize the following principles if he is to become an effective speaker of the word:

1. Language is a basic to revelation.
2. Meaning is a convention dependent upon agreement and commonality of experience among persons.
3. Ability to apprehend the faith follows capacity to comprehend its truths expressed in language.
4. Maturity in faith occasions wider understanding of the language used to express faith, the how as well as the what of revelation.
5. God is the author of meaning at the deepest levels.

## The Preferred Word

Good style in preaching proceeds from an awareness of the distinctions of oral communication contrasted with written expression.[3] While I may reread a difficult passage in an essay, I cannot rehear a part of a sermon I do not understand. My confusion will confirm my preference to be unmoved and unchanged by what I hear. My uncertainty will distance me farther from the speaker and his message as he proceeds.

If clearness is to be achieved, the language the preacher uses must be instantly intelligible, capable of evoking immediate and accurate understanding from the hearer. We choose such language because we recognize the operation of principles which govern word choice in a preaching, speaking situation.
1. Use concrete terms to clarify abstract concepts.
2. Be as specific as possible; avoid generalities.
3. Strive to discover the word most expressive of your idea.
4. Use nouns and verbs aided sparingly by adjectives and adverbs.
5. Describe vividly since description expands the communicative thrust of language well beyond the impact of individual words.
6. Create images which are multisensory expressions of your ideas.
7. Master the metaphor and other stylistic tools.
8. Appraise the effect of the language of your preaching by allowing it to fall upon the ear—how it sounds to you is an important clue to its effect upon others.

We shall examine each of these principles to discover their importance to the development of a clear style, one which possesses, as well, the second hallmark of good preaching, beauty of language.

## Concrete Over Abstract

When we state a preference for concrete expression over the use of abstract words, we do not imply that abstract terms may be eliminated or, indeed, that such elimination is desirable. Abstractions are unavoidable in our use of language. Our concern is to point out that greater ambiguity stems from expression which employs higher and higher levels of abstraction.

The term *Christian* is a high level abstraction which we can trace to a suitable concrete expression, as follows:

Christian
member of a congregation of a recognized denomination
a convinced believer in Christ
a baptized affiliate within a Baptist church
a confessed sinner
a seeker after truth
a young woman
the pastor's daughter
Mary

The statement, "She is a Christian," requires refinement by moving from the high-level abstraction to concrete reality, moving toward specific identity away from generalization.

We can learn much about a person short of knowing specific identity. Observe "she" in the following excerpt from the introduction to a sermon:

> She had listened quietly. Her face betrayed neither agreement nor disagreement. She waited her turn to speak, and then, brushing her hair back with her right hand, she shrugged.

"You know," she said, "I would never believe in a Christ so completely unconcerned about his image...."

She stared without focusing, then sighed, "His could have been such a dramatic life."

What do we know about "she"? She is patient, reserved, unflappable, self-possessed, polite, either neat or she has a nervous habit, right-handed and tends toward the dramatic. The preacher could have introduced her comment with the simple, "a woman said," but she'd be much less a reality to us without the concrete information the first version includes.

Jesus in response to the question, "who is my neighbor?" dealt with the high-level abstraction *neighbor* by presenting the concrete reality who lives even yet as the good Samaritan. The unchanging love of the Father in spite of willfulness away or at home becomes concrete in the story of the prodigal sons. The high-level abstraction receives explicit expression in simple narratives which focus upon concrete reality in action and word.

Preaching which is down to earth may be most expressive of heavenly truth. Abstraction in a discussion of faith is inevitable. However, the clear and beautiful proclamation of the gospel requires the complementary expression of truth in concrete language.

### Be as Specific as Possible; Avoid Generalities

Few of us can escape indictment for dealing in generalities in our hurriedly prepared messages. Ministers prepare from one to three or more sermons each week. The sheer size of our task measured in terms of words prepared to be spoken publicly staggers. Dead-

## The Expressive Basis of Preaching

lines established with excellent intention may be neglected when pastoral or administrative responsibilities keep us from the study.

Unfortunately, preaching in generalities may become more than the occasional lapse when pastoral pressures mount. It can become characteristic of our pulpit presentations; reflecting not merely hurried, but careless preparation. Specificity requires study, research, analysis, and reasoned thought. Generalities can be, and often are, spoken impromptu. There is an important distinction between the truly fluent and the merely glib.

A glib sermon on missions, for example, may offer little more than a loose outline:
  I. Missions: The Command of Christ
  II. Missions: The Challenge to the Church
  III. Missions: The Call to Compassion

The Reverend Mr. Glib alone in his study on a Saturday afternoon will complete the message, relying upon general knowledge. Citations of the Great Commission, the name of his church's missionary organization and, perhaps, a true narrative based upon a missionary's experience gleaned from the heading "missionaries" in an antholgy of illustrations will afford all the specificity he can manage. The great pity is that no one will say to Brother Glib that had he allowed a period of silence after reading each of his major points, most of his hearers could have *thought* a sermon as effective as his, employing general knowledge most of them have available.

On the other hand, a returned missionary can be genuinely fluent fleshing out the same outline. She could describe both command and response to call in terms of personal experience. The challenge we sense in her first-hand experience in language school, in adjustment to culture shock, and in struggles to speak and live the gospel in love in a country of specific geographical, climatic, population, and religious characteristics. Compassion to a youngster named Rhonda who sought medical treatment or William who needed comfort when a flood took his family from him becomes a shared reality. Missions lives in the message of the fluent missionary.

While we cannot have firsthand experience with all areas we should explore in our preaching, we have access to specific information about the ministry and teachings of Jesus, the spread of Christianity, the ancient world, the history of the church, the literature of faith, contemporary society, current events, the Third World, sects, sex, family dissolution, poverty, war—the list is endless.

The minister has been called to a demanding and gratifying task. He cannot preach on topics beyond his reach, but a major part of the challenge he accepts is to extend that reach more and more. He embraces the life of the mind when he accepts the responsibility of proclaiming the gospel. As he prepares to preach, he rummages through the extensive files in his mind. He seeks recall, if not of specific information, the place where such specificity may be reencountered for inclusion in next Sunday's, or better, next month's message.

Mind you, Brother Glib may not do damage other than to his self-respect and the respect he seeks among his parishioners. By ignoring his problem, however, he excludes himself from the company of a pulpit master

## The Expressive Basis of Preaching

such as Paul who might have said, "There is a certain bond between the believer and God which is of indeterminant duration." Instead, he thundered, "For I am sure that neither death, nor life, nor angels nor principalities, nor things present, nor things to come, nor powers, nor height, nor depth, nor anything else in all creation, will be able to separate us from the love of God in Christ Jesus our Lord" (Rom. 8:38-39).

To counter the temptation to deal in generalities, ask of your sermon, What does this message say *specifically* to my hearers? Could they have reached the same conclusions if I had only announced my principal ideas? Have I given particulars upon which they may build yet additional insights? What have I learned as I prepared this message? Will my hearers be learners as I preach it? Is my message fleshed out with the bone and sinew of serious study or with the fat of imprecision and generality?

Admittedly we may encounter resistance to specificity. If we do, we are in good company. When Jesus made Isaiah 61:1-2 an agenda for action in his sermon in Nazareth as he stood poised upon the threshold of his active ministry, the good neighbors and frequenters of the synagogue drove him from their midst (Luke 4:16-30). By this action they said, "Keep it general. Don't bother us with the particulars of ministry." Faithfulness was foremost for Jesus, however. How can we who are to bear witness to him do less?

### Strive to Discover the Word Most Expressive of Your Idea

Most of us have speaking vocabularies larger than our writing vocabularies. The former is often less precise than the latter. The ear may be less discriminating than the eye when we assimilate the meanings of similar-sounding words into our speaking vocabularies. *Allusion*, an indirect reference, is often mistaken for *illusion*, a false perception. *Illusive*, deceptive or unreal, we confuse with *allusive*, something not fully expressed. While *allude* is a verb, it has no counterpart as *illude*, but may be confused with *elude*, to escape. All of us have wrestled with *affect* and *effect; affective* and *effective*. Terms currently confused among otherwise knowledgeable persons are *perimeter*, center boundary, and *parameter*, a mathematical term imprecisely used to suggest the same meaning.[4]

These obviously are examples of the presence in English of homonyms which explained for us, when we were in grade school, our difficulty in using *there* and *their* and *meat* and *meet*. Aided by red marks on papers, we mastered these through using them repeatedly. The examples cited, however, are more sophisticated and their correct use may be illusive. Thus we alluded to them in our discussion of selecting the precise word required for exactness in expression.

Another cautionary note relates to the incidence of supposed synonyms in our language. John A. Broadus whose discussion of style in his *On the Preparation and Delivery of Sermons* continues to be instructive to readers into its second century observed, "The more cultivated a language becomes . . . the more it distinguishes between apparent synonyms."[5] The subtle differences between the following words could be crucial to the exact intention of the preacher to communicate a precise idea:

revelation and inspiration
grace and mercy
compassion and sympathy
true and truth
disciple and apostle
soul and person
salvation and regeneration
holiness and piety
faith and belief
faith and trust
faith and the faith
to instruct and to witness to
preach and teach

Prerequisite to saying exactly what we mean is knowing exactly what we wish to say. There is no substitute for careful consideration of the content of our messages. When content is exact, its expression can be specific, and we can be precise in our selection of the best *word*. Prior to final choice the preacher-craftsman will consider alternative terms and reject all but the most expressive. His will be an informed choice since he will consult standard dictionaries and specialized reference works to aid in his differentiation among possible expressions of the thought.

**Use Nouns and Verbs Aided Sparingly by Adjectives and Adverbs**

If your choice of a noun requires the assistance of an adjective, the noun may be inexact. Verbs which require adverbs may need to be replaced to serve our intention to frame our ideas in the strongest terms.[6] Nouns afford comprehension; verbs provide movement, action.

Through repetition or restatement, the preacher may pile adjective upon adjective, use adverb after adverb (intoning the final *-ly* as in, "we shall hear him carefu*ly*, prayerfu*lly*, eager*ly*, sympathetica*lly*, and enthusiastica*lly*"). He may deem this procedure reenforcement. In reality it may be tedious to hearers capable of discerning the comprehensive meaning of nouns and verbs.

Unless the preacher undergoes the discipline of writing and rewriting, he will probably have no basis for questioning his use of adjectives and adverbs. To improve the style of spoken discourse, the preacher must examine his speech. While listening to a recording may prove helpful, characteristics of usage may remain undetected until the preacher studies a manuscript of his message. A typist may provide a typescript of a recorded message for analysis but that review cannot affect a sermon already preached. Writing the sermon in full or in part prior to its delivery constitutes the principal means of analysis of usage prior to delivery.

Verbs should be active whenever possible. Occasionally the significance of the subject acted upon requires passive construction. First John 1:2 reads, "The life *was made manifest*, and we saw it, and testify to it, and proclaim to you the eternal life which was with the Father and *was made manifest* to us" (authors' italics). We tend, however, to write in the passive voice. We should examine every passive construction to ascertain whether the significance of the subject acted upon is the determinant. Recast the sentence, making the subject the actor. Generally this is the stronger construction. Contrast the vigor of the following:

The withdrawal of John Mark from missionary service was considered by Paul to be sufficient justification for his exclusion from the party of travelers on their return trip to visit the brethren.

Paul considered John Mark's withdrawal from missionary service sufficient justification for excluding him from the party of travelers returning to visit the brethren.

While both statements contain the essential elements, the second clarifies the subject and line of action and reduces the ambiguity of "his." The first is nominal in form—focus upon nouns. The second is verbal, therefore more active and concise.[7]

**Describe to Expand Communication**

The mind's eye sees comprehensively. When we describe the setting, the persons, the actions, the relationships, the emotions in vivid terms, the experiences of our hearers infuse the whole with meaning well beyond the face value of our words. We are artists who paint using language. Those who view our work interpret the images through the breadth and depth of experience they possess. Thus, the impact of the word we speak when we describe may move the hearer profoundly as it touches the strings of memory.

To introduce a sermon based on 2 Corinthians 5:16-21 which begins, "From now on, therefore, we regard no one from a human point of view; even though we once regarded Christ from a human point of view, we regard him thus no longer," the preacher sought to describe a contemporary situation in which this truth has pointed relevance.

A familiar haunt of college students, the small cafe perched precariously on the edge of the campus—an unconscious buffer between town and gown. The moment seemed frozen as the three at the table paused in what their faces revealed was a serious discussion. A ceiling fan stirred the air above, the only movement in the room.

The coffee, forgotten, had grown cold in the thick mugs, their whiteness in marked contrast to the red formica tabletops, the chrome legs. One of the three, a young man, intense, concerned, struggled to be understood. He spoke with a compelling urgency, "I'd like to believe in Christ but. . . ."

Such description stirs the memory of our hearers, calls to consciousness places and experiences stored in the subconscious memory. Each hearer can picture such a place. The details included identify the specific location intended, the unique character of the event described. The preacher includes enough detail to be suggestive, to stimulate recall.

The brush strokes are bold with sufficient detail to afford movement in the direction of the point being made. Too much detail might divert from the point. Without control of the movement of the message to a particular point, the hearer could follow a direction dictated by whimsy, by association with events and places far from the preacher's intention. Thus, the preacher must control his message. His intentionality must not be marred by this or any other attribute of style.

## The Expressive Basis of Preaching

The preacher must cultivate his powers of observation if he is to develop skills in description. He must see life about him. Reality rather than romanticized representations of reality, must become his model. A television situation comedy may be a diversion for the minister, but it is an inferior source for understanding and describing family and other relationships. Serious television programs and films may be helpful but are less meaningful than the direct encounter with actual situations in the hospital, the counseling office, or the homes of church members.

When the preacher finds time for travel and holiday activities, the packing of a notebook to serve as a journal can be a useful means of developing descriptive skills. Away from the press of pastoral and administrative duties, the preacher may, at the end of a busy day, ponder the events and sights he has experienced. While these entries may become sermon illustrations, the exercise should be seen as primarily designed to afford the opportunity to describe, to refine descriptive abilities.

A word of caution about descriptions of events in times past must be added. Inevitably, the preacher will wish to sketch the setting for biblical events—the confrontation of Moses with Pharaoh or the deliverance of Paul and Silas from the prison in Philippi. Careful study of historical material must precede efforts to describe the settings, customs, clothing, and relationships of time past. While some license may be taken, the preacher should use anachronism only intentionally, clearly recognized both by the hearer and the preacher.

## Create Images that Are Multisensory

Imagistic language engages the senses of the hearer.[8] We are all aware that language can bring to mind a vivid visual image. That picturization process may be augmented by appeals to the other senses singly or, more likely, in combination. The visual imagery of the following blends with an appeal to the gustatory sense—the sense of taste: "The family from oldest patriarch with gray beard and hair and lined face to the youngest child with face momentarily lined by the effort to recall, not the escape from Egypt but last year's observance, ate the Passover. Each in his way remembered deliverance. Each tasted the bitter herbs, the younger members in undisguised displeasure; the older, with tears provoked less by the harsh taste of the herbs than by the memory of oppression." The tactile faculty is stirred by recounting how a garment of camel's hair would feel upon the emaciated body of the ascetic John. Martha would bring the sweet, yeasty smell of baking bread from the kitchen to complain of Mary's absence and, in the process, assault our olfactory sense. A light breeze in the cool of the evening, whispering through the trees and lapping at the fringes of the clothing of Jesus and Nicodemus as they talked quietly about a birth from above, stirs our thermal and auditory senses. "One moment the swine were tranquilly indolent; the next, their cursed, cloven hooves were thundering an erratic tattoo in a rush pell-mell down the steep bank and into the lake," stimulates our kinesthetic sense effecting muscle tension and relaxation, and our kinetic sense, response to overt action.

*The Expressive Basis of Preaching* **197**

Preaching in strong, vivid images stirs the senses, heightens interest and aids retention of the idea being shared. The use of such images, however, has the further advantage of giving life to the biblical material which can be experienced through our responding senses. A preaching class intentionally writing with images employed a constant beginning idea: "The tree had what Zacchaeus needed: low limbs." The responses were varied and reflected the wide possibilities available to the imaginative preacher.

The tree had what Zacchaeus needed: low limbs. He was grateful. *Now if they are only strong enough to support me,* he thought, shading his eyes as he peered upward. The sun was directly overhead, a giant candle flame flickering among the leaves. The day was hot, and Zacchaeus welcomed the shadowy coolness of the tree as one welcomes rain on a hot, summer night. *My seat will be the coolest in town,* he laughed quietly, *as well as the highest.* With that thought, he reached up with his dark, wiry arms and grasped the thick, pale-gray limb over his head. The bark felt like the desert, smooth and warm, like cactus and desert brush that dug sharply into his hands. Nevertheless, Zacchaeus leapt upward and swung himself neatly into the leafy coolness of the tree. A few adjustments later, Zacchaeus had a perfect place to watch for Jesus.

The writer of the preceding passage employed strong visual, thermal, tactile, and kinetic images as he described Zacchaeus's ascent to his vantage point. Another added an effective use of olfactory imagery as well as an interesting contemporary phrase to advance the story:

The tree had what Zacchaeus needed: low limbs. He clutched one of the slick limbs and strained to lift his dumpy body. Sweat broke from his forehead as he proceeded to the next branch. "I must get higher," he huffed. Once perched at the chosen spot, he broke several of the branches which emitted a pungent odor. His eyes strained to find the teacher among the crowd. "Here he comes," shouted a storekeeper. Zacchaeus leaned forward for a better look and was as surprised as a contestant on *The Price Is Right* when Jesus said, "Come on down."

Another stem designed for the stimulation of imagistic writing, "As Jesus waded into the muddy waters of the Jordan," evoked the following student response:

As Jesus waded into the muddy waters of the Jordan, the mud felt soft and smooth against his feet. His robe clung to his knees as it gained weight from the water. The sun's reflection off the water made his eyes squint. Finally, as the water raced to his chest, he stopped in front of a man whose face was glowing. John the Baptist had known this time would come. Now, as the warm water flowed around them and made their robes billow, John placed his hands on Jesus and gently lowered him into the murky water.

While the preacher will undoubtedly employ imagistic expression more often in narrative than in other sermon forms, he should recognize that any story will be strengthened through the heightened vividness occasioned by conscious imaging. Introductions, conclusions, illustrations, even specific instances, may gain and sustain attention readily when the senses are stirred by the language of the preacher.

*The Expressive Basis of Preaching* 199

## Master the Metaphor and Other Stylistic Tools

The discovery of comparisons is an integral element of understanding. We give directions "Go like you're going to City Park, but turn on Maple." We describe: "He drives like a man possessed." We ask, "Is it like the gear box on a tractor?" Comparisons are in our folk ways and folk memory: "He's wise as an owl." Or, "she's bright as a penny." Colorful language contains many expressions where comparison is explicit, unexplained but immediately comprehended: "lucky stiff," "green thumb," "stubborn mule," or "wet blanket."

Such colorful idioms are assimilated unconsciously as a part of our store of expressive tools. We use them readily without realizing that they are stylistic devices. They are figurative language aiding our colorful expression of ideas. We use them naturally until they are defined for us as a part of good style. We immediately assume that they are "arty" and must be avoided. What of value, after all, would we lose? Much of our language in hymns would be gone.

"A Mighty Fortress Is Our God"—a metaphor
"Thy Word Is Like a Garden, Lord"—a simile
"Thou burning sun with golden beam . . . O praise Him"—personification
"O Zion, Haste"—personification
"Sun of My Soul, Thou Saviour Dear"—a metaphor
"O Little Town of Bethlehem"—personification
"Rock of Ages, Cleft for Me"—a metaphor
"Like a River Glorious Is God's Perfect Peace"—simile

To abandon figurative language would deprive us of much Scripture.

"Ye are the salt of the earth . . . . the light of the world" (Matt. 5:13-14, KJV)—metaphors

"He is like a tree planted by streams of water. . . . The wicked . . . are like chaff which the wind drives away" (Ps. 1:3-4)—similes

"O Death, where is thy victory? O Death where is thy sting?" (1 Cor. 15:55)—personification; apostrophe

"For as in Adam all die, so also in Christ shall all be made alive" (1 Cor. 15:22)—metonymy

"For you know the grace of our Lord Jesus Christ, that though he was rich, yet for your sake he became poor, so that by his poverty you might become rich" (2 Cor. 8:9)—antimetabole

"There is one body and one Spirit, just as you were called to the one hope that belongs to your call, one Lord, one faith, one baptism, one God and Father of us all, who is above all and through all and in all" (Eph. 4:4-6)—anaphora

Thus, we find abundant evidence of figures of speech in the language of the faith—our hymns and our Bible. There should be no surprise when we encounter figurative language within the verbal expression of faith: We thereby expand the capability of language to express the difficult, if not inexpressible, concepts at the heart of revealed Truth. Jesus used language in the manner of the pioneers of faith before him. His diction is that of the Old Testament, altered by the unique perspective he brought to bear upon the issues and concerns of his day. As teacher he employed the verbal means at his disposal to condense Truth into memorable metaphor and to expand its relevance through parable. That the church preserved his words until they could be set down in the

Gospels testifies to their apt and, therefore, memorable content.

Attention to figures of speech in treatments of preaching are less than extensive. Revisions of the John A. Broadus text in this century have reduced from three to none the figures of speech recommended for their impact upon elegance in style. The revision by Jesse Burton Weatherspoon in 1944[9] included consideration of simile, metaphor, and personification—the three deemed most useful by Broadus in 1870. They were omitted from the 1979 edition[10] revised by Vernon L. Stanfield. However, Elizabeth Achtemeier, *Creative Preaching: Finding the Words*,[11] published in 1980 and one of the few efforts to treat style meaningfully currently available in the literature of preaching, discusses pictorial language and in particular recognizes the power of the metaphor and simile.

Perhaps two values from recognition of the presence of figures of speech in our verbal expression need to be considered: First, they are relevant for biblical interpretation since their presence in the text can affect our understanding of passages which employ them; second, they afford a means for assessing correctness in expression when they are employed either consciously or unconsciously. People think and speak in metaphors and employ other stylistic devices naturally. Their presence in utterance may be less a literary conceit in our age than an indication that our use of language stems from the reality that this is the way words work.

Among the figures of speech recognized as most helpful to the preacher, then, are the following:

1. *Metaphor:* a figure of speech which implies similarity between two different things.

"Thy Word is a lamp to my feet, and a light to my path" (Ps. 119:105).

2. *Simile:* a comparison of conditions or objects alike only in certain particulars.

"For he grew up before him like a young plant, and like a root out of dry ground" (Isa. 53:2).

3. *Personification:* affording personal qualities to inanimate things or abstract ideas.

"The heavens are telling the glory of God; and the firmament proclaims his handiwork. Day to day pours forth speech, and night to night declares knowledge" (Ps. 19:1-2).

4. *Hyperbole:* a figure which exaggerates or dramatically diminishes.

"Though your sins are like scarlet, they shall be as white as snow" (Isa. 1:18).

5. *Paradox:* an affirmation of a truth that appears contradictory.

"Because we look not to the things that are seen but to the things that are unseen; for the things that are seen are transient, but the things that are unseen are eternal" (2 Cor. 4:18).

6. *Anaphora:* the repetition of a word or words at the beginning of successive clauses in a sentence.

"Finally, brethren, whatever is true, whatever is honorable, whatever is just, whatever is pure, whatever is lovely, whatever is gracious, if there is any excellence, if there is anything worthy of praise, think about these things" (Phil. 4:8).

7. *Antimetabole:* repetition in successive clauses in reverse grammatical order.

"For if you live according to the flesh you will die, but if by the Spirit you put to death the deeds of the body you will live" (Rom. 8:13).

8. *Hypotyposis:* a very lively and vivid description.

"Are they servants of Christ? I am a better one—I am talking like a madman—with far greater labors, far more imprisonments, with countless beatings, and often near death. Five times I have received at the hands of the Jews the forty lashes less one. Three times I have been beaten with rods; once I was stoned. Three times I have been shipwrecked; a night and a day I have been adrift at sea; on frequent journeys, in danger from rivers, danger from robbers, danger from my own people, danger from Gentiles, danger in the city, danger in the wilderness, danger at sea, danger from false brethren; in toil and hardship; through many a sleepless night, in hunger and thirst, often without food, in cold and exposure. And apart from other things, there is the daily pressure upon me of my anxiety for all the churches" (2 Cor. 11:23-28).

9. *metonoymy:* a part becomes an expression of the whole.

"O Jerusalem, Jerusalem, killing the prophets and stoning those who are sent to you! How often would I have gathered your children together as a hen gathers her brood under her wings and you would not!" (Luke 13:34).

10. *oxymoron:* joining two usually contradictory terms.

"For though I am *free* from all men, I have made myself a *slave* to all, that I might win the more" (1 Cor. 9:19 authors' italics).

Like any other craftsman, the wordsmith knows the tools that are available for his use. A recognition of figures of speech is the first step to our appreciation of their worth and development of the capability to employ them. Obviously we may overwork any of these stylistic devices. To stack metaphor upon metaphor would achieve the effect opposite to that sought—we would diminish our effectiveness as communicators. The advice "use figurative language sparingly" if read "not at all" is a mistaken notion. Work to achieve the most expressive way of saying what you must say. Since expression which comes from the depths of both our perception and desire to preach will represent the struggle to combine thought and language meaningfully, we will find ourselves employing language naturally using figures of speech. Rather than suppress figurative language, learn to use it to heighten your capability to say meaningfully that which can never be said easily.

A word of caution: Avoid mixing metaphors. To say that "John the Baptist blazed a trail over a sea of religious misconceptions" may be merely confusing or outright humorous. Further, fresh modes of expression must supplant the inevitable cliché which comes first to mind. "Game of life" and "vale of tears" are expressions bankrupt in impact through overuse.

## How Language Sounds Matters

Appraise the effect of the language of your preaching by allowing it to fall upon the ear—how it sounds to you is an important clue to its effect upon others. Reading your material aloud while you prepare it aids not only your assessment of its aural impact upon others but also helps your preparation for delivery by giving you added familiarity with the language you will employ. The ear, as well, is attuned to hear grammatical errors or to discover cumbersome statement. Thus, rewriting is facilitated by reading aloud.[12]

We are conscious, as well, that sounds can enhance our expression of ideas. The overuse of *alliteration* in preaching causes some restraint in discussing its legitimate use as a device to afford reiteration to ideas being expressed. When repetition of the same sound is a natural expression of the sense of the text, alliteration is altogether appropriate.[13] Too often, however, two concepts lead immediately to alliterative statements while the third must be forced into an acceptably similar expression. Or worse, suppose the text is the Great Commission (Matt. 28:19-20). Consideration of the final phrase "and lo, I am with you always, to the close of the age" offers the one-word statement of the concluding concept, "Presence." That is a reasonable choice. Let that expression dictate how the other divisions of the text will be identified. "All authority in heaven and on earth has been given to me." seems clearly summarized in *authority*. That almost means "Prestige," however, so let's go with that. The verbal forms following demand action: *go, make disciples, baptizing, teaching*. They require summarization in a nominal form to follow alliteratively the others. These are ways faith is promoted; thus, "promotion."

> The Great Commission
> I. Prestige
> II. Promotion
> III. Presence

That rendering is most unfortunate because authority and prestige barely agree and are by no means synonyms. Promotion would require elaborate justification which could obscure the point finally stated. While presence is a valid statement of the third concept, it proves a harsh taskmaster in dictating the statement of the two ideas which precede it.

> The Great Commission
> I. Jesus affirmed his authority.
> II. Jesus described our mission.
> III. Jesus promised his presence.

While such an outline makes use of alliteration within the points, the expression seems natural and not contrived. This is an important distinction for inclusion of alliteration in the expression of a sermon outline. Forced or contrived alliteration should be restated.

*Assonance,* repetition of a dominant or concluding vowel or, perhaps, vowel and consonant combination, is a second reiterative tool: A message based on Romans 12:2, "Do not be *conformed* to this world but be *transformed* by the renewal of your mind, that you may prove what is the will of God, what is good and acceptable and perfect" (authors' italics), could have two points summarized by the words, *conformed* and *transformed.* The use of these would afford reiteration through assonance.

*Repetition of a key term* will also aid in audience comprehension and recall of sermon content. The key term, *marks,* from Galatians 6:17, "Henceforth let no man trouble me; for I bear on my body the marks of Jesus," could make use of this reiterative pattern:

> I. The marks of Jesus emanate from within; He is within us.
> II. The marks of Jesus indicate ownership; we are His.

III. The marks of Jesus validate our service; His will is ours.

"Emanate, indicate, and validate" are examples of terms with assonance. The repetition of "marks" builds upon a key concept. The similar form of each principal division of the sermon reflects the fourth reiterative pattern, *parallelism*. Thus, the preacher may aid hearer understanding by using appropriate reiterative patterns based on the following:
1. Alliteration
2. Assonance
3. Repetition of a key term
4. Parallelism

The language of the sermon must be instantly intelligible. There is no chance to rehear the spoken word. Its impact must be immediate. If the hearer requires definition or explanation, it must be offered at once. The preparation of a complete manuscript leads often to the use of nontalking language, language suited better to the formal paper than to the sermon. We write to impress our readers with the significance of our ideas by stating them in structures that are complex, in words often esoteric if not obtuse. We are wrong, but we cling tenaciously to that misunderstanding. If we "write out" our sermons, they frequently sound stiff and uncommunicative.

If we should avoid nontalking language, how shall we preach in talking terms immediately intelligible to our hearers? Follow these guidelines:
1. Use clear, simple, easy to follow sentences which hold together grammatically.
2. Avoid the elaborate term; show preference for the simple expression of your idea.

3. Don't seek to impress by using jargon—a specialized vocabulary as incomprehensible to the unitiated as the mysterious, special understandings of the Gnostics.
4. Do employ the patterns of conversational address.
5. Contractions may be used in sermons since they contribute to the natural flow of speech.
6. Personal pronouns, including first-person pronouns, are acceptable, much preferred over the circumlocutions (beating around the bush) required to avoid them.
7. Get to the point; avoid restating the obvious and explaining the known.
8. Beware the verbal stall: "It is apparent that. . . ." or "What I would like to say about that is. . . ."
9. Employ all the channels of communication available for your use: The message is multisensory appealing to ear, eye, and, through imagery, the other senses.
10. Use language interestingly and comfortably. Your hearers' attention will be captivated by skillful use of language. Whatever you say or however you express a concept in your sermon, you must be comfortable with that expression. Otherwise you will sound stilted.

**A Paradox: Enhance Oral Style Through Writing**

Preparation of the sermon leads to the act of preaching—spoken discourse. If the mode of presentation preferred by the preacher is manuscript or memory, the full text of the sermon will be prepared. The minister will preach the manuscript in either case. The full range

## The Expressive Basis of Preaching

of energetic involvement must be called into play. He shall know the sermon beyond the words on the page because he originated the idea, allowed it to germinate, watered, and fertilized it through prayer, study, interpretation, and development, urged form upon it and finally captured it in a manuscript in language designed for oral presentation.

The preacher who prefers an extemporaneous mode of presentation engages in the same comprehensive preparation as the minister who preaches from manuscript or memory except that he does not prepare a full manuscript. Instead, he begins to develop the probable means for expressing the ideas of the sermon through writing out portions of the message such as the introduction, the conclusion, or, perhaps, an illustration he has selected. Or, following the outline he may speak the concepts of a portion of the sermon aloud until he feels the expression captures his intention.

The crucial determinant of success in development of language for preaching from memory, manuscript, or outline (extemporaneous delivery) is the structure of the message which emerges from the text to provide the spine of the sermon. This cohesive force will expedite the development of the sermon as writing continues or as the preacher orally selects language to flesh out the outline. In both approaches, the preacher must "hear" the message as he selects the phrases and sentences which make up the sermon.

By definition, extemporaneous preachers defer specific word choice until the time of delivery. But that selection is informed by experimentation with language as a form of oral message which comes into being and achieves a degree of stability awaiting the preacher's presentation when the dynamic factors in the communicative situation influence his specific choice of words.

## Your Style

We began this discussion by defining style in part as the distinctive expressive power characteristic of the preacher. The development of good style occurs slowly through careful effort. It awaits specific attention to detail in expression. The preacher hears in John's prologue of the beginning as Word. The Word made flesh inspires the preacher to be an instrument for reincarnating the Word through the language he uses. Such a magnificent task calls forth the best from us as persons called through the Word to express the Word completely, winsomely, lovingly with telling effect. And there is great joy when through the power of the Spirit we discern that the Word has again been reenlivened. Amen.

## Think on These Things

1. Explore the concept: "God as *person* who *reveals* in *language* is the basic understanding essential to faith."
2. Study the sermons of a preacher you admire to determine whether the language he employs is instantly intelligible. Develop examples which you feel corroborate your assessment.
3. In a sermon manuscript or text, study the preacher's use of abstract language. Are there efforts to express these concepts in concrete language? Provide examples.

4. Differentiate among *articulate, fluent, literate,* and *glib.*
5. By definitions you formulate, express the subtle shades of difference between the two almost synonyms on page 191.
6. Examine a sermon for use of the passive voice. If the sense will permit, reword the examples you discover using the active voice.
7. Try your hand at imagistic language by completing the following based on Isaiah 6: "Isaiah felt as though his senses were bombarded. . . ."
8. Exercise your descriptive powers by completing the following: "Paul pitched forward on the sun-hardened surface of the road to Damascus. . . ."
9. Find examples in sermons for each stylistic device discussed in this chapter. Which are easiest to find? Most difficult? (Use the language of the sermon, not the Scriptures cited.)
10. Find examples of strained alliteration in sermons available on tape or in print. Of nontalking language. Of creative and effective use of language.

## Suggested Reading

Benson, Thomas W., Prosser, Michael H. *Readings in Classical Rhetoric.* Boston: Allyn and Bacon, Inc., 1969.

Campbell, Paul. *The Speaking and the Speakers of Literature.* Belmont, California: Dickenson Publishing Co., Inc., 1967.

Corbett, Edward P. J. *Classical Rhetoric for the Modern Student.* New York: Oxford University Press, 1965.

Hoefler, Richard Carl. *Creative Preaching and Oral Writing.* The C.S.S. Publishing Co., Inc., n.d.

Lambuth, David. *The Golden Book on Writing*. New York: The Viking Press, 1963.

Nichols, Sue. *Words on Target*. Richmond, Virginia: John Knox Press, 1967.

Thonssen, Lester; Baird, A. Craig; Braden, Waldo W. *Speech Criticism*. New York: The Ronald Press Co., 1970.

### Notes

1. Polly Hargis Dillard, "Children and Worship," *Review and Expositor*, 80 (Spring 1983); 263.
2. A failure to accept the differentiation between word and reality behind the word may be at the heart of much confusion regarding biblical interpretation. Symbol is less the issue in meaning than the reality it arbitrarily represents in language whether the language be biblical or a translation—but particularly in the latter case.
3. Wayne C. Minnick, *Public Speaking* (Boston: Houghton Mifflin Company, 1979), p. 145 *ff*, presents an interesting discussion of the nature of language for speech contrasted with language in written communication.
4. The confusion regarding *perimeter* and *parameter* has made its way into educational circles where *parameter* has almost completely usurped the place of *perimeter* when the latter clearly is the word and sense intended.
5. John A. Broadus, *A Treatise on the Preparation and Delivery of Sermons*, ed. Edwin Charles Dargan (New York: A. C. Armstrong and Son, 1980), p. 368-369.
6. William Strunk, Jr., and E. B. White, *The Elements of Style*, 3rd ed. (New York: Macmillan Publishing Co., Inc., 1979), p. 71.
7. Jane Blankenship, *A Sense of Style* (Belmont, Cal.: Dickenson Publishing Company, Inc., 1968), p. 94.
8. A study of imagistic language in courses in oral reading of literature provides the basis for this discussion. A standard textbook which we recommend as particularly helpful is that of Charlotte I. Lee, *Oral Interpretation* (Atlanta: Houghton Mifflin Company, 1971), p. 189 *ff*.
9. John A. Broadus, *On the Preparation and Delivery of Sermons*, revised by J. B. Weatherspoon (New York: Harper and Brothers, 1944).
10. John A. Broadus, *On the Preparation and Delivery of Sermons*, revised by Vernon L. Stanfield (San Francisco: Harper and Row Publishers, 1979).
11. Elizabeth Achtemeier, *Creative Preaching: Finding the Words* (Nashville: Abingdon, 1980).
12. Compare the discussion of the oral manuscript in Clyde Fant, *Preaching for Today*, (New York: Harper and Row, 1975), p. 118.
13. Blankenship, p. 79.

# 9

# The Communicative Basis of Preaching

All the efforts of the preacher to prepare a word to proclaim lead to the pulpit. The word must be spoken. The sermon must be preached. The preacher is a communicator who uses the ordinary tools of everyday speech to accomplish an extraordinary task: to proclaim a word from God.

## The Preacher as Communicator

The task of the preacher is verbal. He listens, he reads, he writes, and he *speaks*. While we have made it clear that the antecedents of speaking are crucial to the preacher's success in his craft, his skills as a communicator are inextricably tied to the congregation's apprehension of the message which has emerged through his extensive preparation.

The message of the preacher comes to the congregation of hearers as signals perceived by the eye and the ear. What we see and hear shapes attitude and response. We willingly appropriate new information, accept a rekindling of old ideas, become convinced, and are persuaded to action through the intentional and unintentional messages we receive as members of a congregation.

The preacher who communicates effectively the message, carefully prepared, strives to make the presentation of his sermon correspond as completely as possible with the content he has prepared. To do this, unintentional negative signals must be reduced; intentional positive communicative elements in the presentation of the message must be strengthened.

### It's No Business Like Show Business

On occasion the significance of our task, its overwhelming character, makes us feel that the humble skills of the preacher are inevitably ineffective. They can't measure up to the weight of the word we bear. We confuse that weight with ours and assume we must be a heavyweight ourselves if the word is to be effective as spoken. We fall, thus, into the practice of intoning rather than telling, wailing rather than witnessing, whining and chanting rather than speaking directly and vigorously the joyous good news.[1]

We may feel a necessity to employ a special pulpit voice. We engage in a preaching demeanor which is unlike the behavior which our friends and colleagues observe in our nonpreaching activity. It is not enough that we use a specialized vocabulary; we distort our words through over-enunciation (and the occasional correction of a supposed error in grammar, "God calls you and I," and pronunciation of *sin* as *sen*) or through modified stress patterns (such as the distortion which occurs when too much stress is placed on the first syllable of the name of our Lord, as in Jeee-zus).

Our bewildered congregations who tune out for a time of essential respite from the unrelieved torrent of sound are justified in an unguarded response upon tuning back in, "My word! He's abandoned English altogether." Should that occur there need be no embarrassment in the discovery of an error. Such behaviors—the pulpit voice, a special demeanor, and unusual pronunciation—give rise to a mistrust of the ordinary processes of communication as capable of bearing the weight of the Word the preacher wishes to present. The setting of polished pulpit and cushioned pews, of crystal chandelier and imported stained glass, of hymns and anthems, of solemn words and inspired Word, of prayer and praise seems to create an environment which demands resonance, lowered pitch, heightened breathiness, elevated diction, pristine pronunciation, and artistry of gesture, even when these are forced communication behaviors.

Or, another context for preaching is reminiscent of a pep rally with cheers and fight songs, typically characterized by a studied informality, a structured spontaneity, a frenetic striving for warmth in fellowship, a rhythmic crescendo pointing expectantly toward the first words of the preacher. All of this buildup may call forth from the preacher a response that attempts to fulfill the expectancy generated. Ordinary speech seems pale and insipid in contrast to what seems to be called for.

While these may be perceived as extreme cases, both may be encountered. Each may be the means by which the preacher is trapped into speaking and acting in ways which may focus more upon his skills in adaptation to the circumstances than to his faithful proclamation of the Word of truth.

The immediate antecedents of preaching must facilitate the preacher's response: a direct, forceful speaking of the Word unencumbered by artificiality which may diminish the demands of the gospel. Does the setting for the sermon inevitably pose such a dilemma? Certainly not when the context is viewed as an appropriate setting for the speaking and hearing of the Word. While we no longer regard the sermon as the only means by which worship may be deemed worthy, nevertheless the sermon is a significant element within those planned as service to God. For that reason the ministers in planning the service must carefully construct an appropriate setting for the speaking of the message which will enhance that Word spoken reasonably and well.[2]

What we are about is not show business. If we confuse the weight of the Word with ours, our reaction may be to *act* as though we indeed do bear that weight. The preacher, however, is no actor; proclamation is no business like show business.

All of us know that the authenticity of the Word we speak lies not in our speaking but in the Holy Spirit who mediates the Word through our words spoken and heard in faith. Not only is this partnership between minister and Holy Spirit essential, it cannot be fabricated by even the most well-meaning religious speaker who strives to get the words right, to reconstruct the emotional coloration, to recreate the sounds and sights of preaching. That utterance will only ring true when the Holy Spirit does his work with that of his preacher partner.

## The Models of Preaching

Blessed is the preacher who has found models which preserve the best of pulpit skill! Unconsciously or

## The Communicative Basis of Preaching

consciously we are affected in our preaching by our definitions of the art assimilated through the observation of others who have preached to us. Many of these models possess characteristics we would do well to pattern our pulpit ministries after. Some, however, need careful evaluation. Certain characteristics may have served former generations well but no longer reflect the best means of communicating to this generation. Occasionally our models genuinely and effectively communicated to a social or economic grouping different from that we are called upon to serve. But choices of models may be nonevaluative. The assimilation of these characteristics may not foster our best service.

Ignoring the fact that television is predominantly an entertainment medium—a fact not lost upon the TV preacher—the contemporary minister may adopt a successful television figure as his model for pulpit speech and action. A robed clergyman with sweeping gestures and well-modulated voice; a chatty, cliché-ridden master of ceremonies who harnesses the talk-show format for profit; an impresario presiding over a well-oiled religious organization; or a glib con artist purveying a nationalistic faith which is trouble free and success oriented are among the possible models available to today's preacher. But to follow such models is to make the pulpit a stage for our acting out what we determine preaching to be based upon our choice of models.

While it may be argued that good comes from such presentations, it must be acknowledged that the pulpit of the local church is no place for TV simulation. The sermon is not an entertaining monologue. We derive the authenticity of the word we speak from our personal encounter with that Word and its impact upon us. Our response is unique; our statement of that impact is ours, expressed in terms of our personality with our voices and that movement we are comfortable with.

The models we follow should possess these characteristics:

1. They must be genuine and sincere.
2. Their emotional response to the gospel must be varied: To be intensely angry or persistently Pollyannaish are red flags not to be ignored.
3. Our models must affect our apprehension of the gospel. We should analyze our responses to discover what communicative attributes have spoken to us for good.
4. Our models should serve as guides to our particular response to the demands of our vocation. A composite of attributes from several models may be useful in sharpening our skills along the lines of effective communication we perceive as characteristic of these models.
5. Snap assessments may be misleading: Observe over a period of time those whose ministries may become a pattern for us. If possible, come to know them personally and discover the depths of spiritual commitment from which they minister.
6. Do not ignore the models found in the pages of the New Testament or in church history.

Good models and an appreciation for our unique capabilities for the task to which we are called should enable us to discover attributes which will foster the presentation of our messages with effectiveness and effect.

## Verbal Communication: The Use of Voice[3]

The sermon is primarily a message spoken and heard. The preacher should cultivate good voice production habits to assure his speaking well when he preaches his sermons. In order to train his voice for its best use as a tool of communication, the preacher must understand something of voice production. To some extent a careful training of the ear must accompany such understanding in order for the preacher to discern when he is using his voice to the best of his capability.

### Phonation: The Production of Speech Sounds

Sound for speech originates in the larynx or voice box housed in the throat (pharynx). Inside the larynx are the vocal folds—two folds of tissue anchored to each end, capable of relaxation and tension. When we breathe deeply, the vocal folds separate to allow free passage of air into and out of the lungs. When we have the urge to speak, the folds are drawn together with appropriate tenseness. The expelled column of air sets the folds into vibration originating the nonrefined speech sound basic to our production of words. Among the factors which control the nature of the sound that we make are, the following:
1. The length of the vocal folds
2. Their density
3. Their tension
4. The presence of foreign matter, infection, or growths in the area of the vocal folds
5. The overall adjustment and well-being of the speaker.

Obviously we have no control over the physical characteristics of our vocal folds, that is, their length and density. Appropriate tenseness is required for the correct vibration of these folds of tissue.

When our adjustment to the speaking situation is poor—when we are nervous or apprehensive—we may find our overall tension to affect adversely the tension in the vocal folds, causing our voices to reflect a strident tone or a higher than normal pitch level. We may attempt to overcome the diminished effectiveness of our voices by forcing the tone through speaking too loudly. Should we ignore the causes of such faults in voice production, we could become hoarse and damage the vocal folds themselves. This may result over a period of time in chronic hoarseness or the development of speaker's nodes which necessitates surgery or complete rest of the voice to correct the problem. Again, the use of the voice when a cold or other infection is aggravating hoarseness can cause long-lasting damage to the voice-producing mechanism.

**Breathing for Speech**

As we have observed, speech sounds originate in the larynx when the vocal folds are set into vibration by the movement of air from the lungs. The diaphragm, the muscle which serves as a partition to separate the chest cavity from the abdomen, is the chief muscle of breathing. In its relaxed position it is shaped like an inverted bowl. When the diaphragm contracts, it flattens, expanding the space within the chest cavity. Air rushes in; we have inhaled. Relaxation of the diaphragm reduces the space. Air is forced out; we have exhaled.

## The Communicative Basis of Preaching

When we have the urge to speak, speech sounds are made by the action of the exhaled column of air which sets the vocal folds into vibration. The preacher should observe the natural breathing of a small, sleeping child to observe the rise and fall of the abdomen indicating the normal movement of the diaphragm in breathing at rest. Our breathing for speech should be centered similarly in the lower chest cavity. Diaphragmatic-abdominal breathing is best suited to the production of speech for the following reasons:
1. Control of breathing is enhanced.
2. Support of the tone through the ends of phrases is facilitated.
3. The possibility of reciprocal tension stemming from muscular tension in the upper chest (as, for example, in clavicular breathing) is reduced.

Consciousness of the method of diaphragmatic abdominal breathing may be developed by using the following technique:
1. Stand in a relaxed, erect posture.
2. Place your open hand, palm toward your body, fingers splayed, on your abdomen.
3. Take a deep breath forcing your hand forward through the movement of the lower chest's expansion.
4. Slowly exhale. Feel the movement of your hand toward your body as the volume of air in the lungs is diminished.
5. Inhale. Count slowly and vigorously from one to ten. Repeat the exercise, but this time count as though each number were a command that required immediate obedience. Each forceful com-

mand should substantially reduce the volume of air in your lungs. How many commands can you give?
6. Inhale. Count slowly from one to ten (or beyond) as though each number were an instruction patiently explained to a child. The expenditure of air for each number should enable you to support the tone for many "instructions." How many did you give?
7. When next you sing with a group (congregation or choir), concentrate upon diaphragmatic-abdominal breathing. Experiment with lengthening the phrases supported by a single inhalation—a procedure which will be unnoticed in congregational singing.
8. When you inhale for all of these exercises, consciously avoid movement in the shoulders or upper chest. Such movement indicates the probability of clavicular breathing. Remember: When you breath for speech, movement should be substantially in the area of the diaphragm.

**Breathing Faults in Voice Production**

When the preacher fails to breathe deeply enough to support the tone through the logical breaks at the ends of phrases, a choppy, awkward flow of communication results. The preacher must engage both his mind, to ensure the flow of complete thoughts, and breath support to provide sufficient volume and vigor to the expression of ideas. Shallow breathing will contribute to short, erratic phrasing.

Occasionally too much breath is expended in the production of sounds resulting in *breathiness*. The preacher may thus have a feathery edge to his words,

*The Communicative Basis of Preaching* 223

particularly those composed of sounds that are produced principally by *breath:* the fricative consonants [f-v], [θ-ð], [s-z], [ʃ-ʒ], [h].[4]
Read the following Scripture from Colossians 1:15-20 (NIV) until you are familiar with the language. Record the passage. Listen carefully to the fricative consonants as you play the recording back. Is there too much hissing on the fricative sounds? Do you note any whistling accompanying the [s] sounds? Reread the passage striving for economy of breath.

> He is the image of the invisible God, the firstborn over all creation. For by him all things were created: things in heaven and on earth, visible and invisible, whether thrones or powers or rulers or authorities; all things were created by him and for him. He is before all things, and in him all things hold together. And he is the head of the body, the church; he is the beginning and the firstborn from among the dead, so that in everything he might have the supremacy. For God was pleased to have all his fullness dwell in him, and through him to reconcile to himself all things, whether things on earth or things in heaven, by making peace through his blood, shed on the cross.

**The Production of Voice**

To understand the production of voice, the following procedure may be followed:
1. Place the upper side of the right hand just below the lower surface of the jaw. The thumb should be relaxed and out of the way.
2. Gently apply pressure with the forefinger against the neck. You will feel a structure we frequently refer to as the Adam's apple, the larynx.

3. Swallow. The larynx will rise and then resume its former position.
4. Now that you have found the larynx, explore its front exterior surface with your thumb and forefinger.
5. Hold your thumb and forefinger in place resting lightly upon the anterior surface (front) of the larynx. You are holding the thyroid cartilage which serves to protect the vocal folds from a frontal blow. The interior surface of this cartilage provides one attachment of the vocal folds.
6. Produce the sound [z], the initial sound in zoo. You should feel the vibration required to produce this sound through your thumb and forefinger. Now, say the word *zoo* and sustain the vowel sound. You will be able to feel vibrations resulting from the production of the consonant [z] and the vowel [u], spelled in the case *oo*.

**Phonation Faults in Voice Production**

The faults of voice production which occur in the larynx, then, are breathiness (see above), harshness or stridency, hoarseness or raspiness, glottal shock (a hiccup-like sound that may occur on an initial vowel) and a habitual pitch level unsuited to the size of the vibrating body—a pitch level too low or too high.

The preacher should strive to identify what has been styled the optimum pitch: that pitch level at which voice production occurs with greatest ease and communicative effect. The trained ear is the best aid to the discovery of the optimum pitch level for your voice. You should cultivate an ability to vary pitch levels in keeping with

*The Communicative Basis of Preaching* 225

the sense of the message. Take, for example, Psalm 150: the mood is joyous, the language captures varied responses to the praise offered to God in worship.

> Praise the Lord!
>
> Praise God in his sanctuary;
> praise him in his mighty firmament!
> Praise him for his mighty deeds;
> praise him according to his exceeding greatness!
>
> Praise him with trumpet sound;
> praise him with lute and harp!
> Praise him with timbrel and dance;
> praise him with strings and pipe!
> Praise him with sounding cymbals;
> praise him with loud clashing cymbals!
>
> Let everything that breathes praise the Lord!
> Praise the Lord!

Record the reading of this psalm as you consciously express the many and varied ways of expressing joyous praise. Read the psalm many times as you strive for wider and still wider expression of praise. As you listen to your recording, note those pitch levels where the voice seems to your ear to communicate best. Ask a partner to listen to you. Can you agree that one level seems best for your voice? Change the reading to Psalm 102 where the mood is introspective and solemn. Read and reread; listen. Try to sense those pitch levels which seem best for your voice.

A second means for discovering your optimum pitch is to use a piano and quietly match pitches with a sustained sung tone to discover the lowest comfortable pitch and the highest. These limits constitute your pitch range from lowest to highest. Count the notes on the piano. Approximately one-third of the way from the lowest pitch to the highest in your range should be near your optimum pitch level. If your voice tires easily, if you become hoarse consistently when you preach, or if you seem to utilize pitch levels in which variety lower or higher seems impossible, you must give attention to finding and using your optimum pitch level.

**Resonation: The Quality of Your Voice**

The phonated sound is immediately amplified and enriched by the process we describe as resonation. The quality of voice added to the phonated sound is resonance. We can understand the effect of resonance through an analogy comparing voice production with the playing of a violin. The string could be suspended from one point to another in mid air. The bow could be drawn across it. The sound would be minimal. Place the string over the carefully crafted instrument, set it into vibration through drawing the bow across it, and the resonance-producing cavity beneath it will transform the sound into the music we associate with that instrument. The tone present in the vibrating string is now amplified and enriched by the resonating cavity which is the principal source of the sound we hear and interpret as music of the violin.

Each of us possesses a vibrating body of a particular size with characteristics which make up our vocal identity. Also, we have resonating cavities which produce the unique sound that our friends recognize when after years of absence we call them on the telephone. They know our particular sound and recognize our voices. Generally, what they recognize is

## The Communicative Basis of Preaching

the characteristic resonance or quality they associate with us.

There are three principal resonating cavities: 1. The throat or pharyngeal cavity; 2. The mouth or the oral cavity; 3. The nose or the nasal cavity. Resonance faults may result from tension; too much tension generally will affect the interior surfaces of the cavities (particularly the throat and mouth) with the result that higher overtones are amplified and the voice takes on the characteristic of stridency alluded to already. Too much resonance gives the voice a nasal quality we find unpleasant. Too little nasal resonance results in a muffled sound similar to that produced with too much nasal resonation. The former characteristic we call nasality or hypernasality; the latter is denasality or hyponasality.

Again, the trained ear is required to identify and address resonance faults. Record the following passage from Colossians 4:2-6.

> Continue steadfastly in prayer, being watchful in it with thanksgiving; and pray for us also, that God may open to us a door for the word, to declare the mystery of Christ, on account of which I am in prison, that I may make it clear, as I ought to speak. Conduct yourselves wisely toward outsiders, making the most of the time. Let your speech always be gracious, seasoned with salt, so that you may know how you ought to answer every one.

Paul here gave advice. Read the passage through several times in order to grasp the full significance of what he was saying. Now, give the advice as you read and record the passage. Replay your recording, listening to the following words: *continue, thanksgiving, may, mystery, on account, am, prison, may make, conduct, making, most, time, may know, answer, one*. Each of these words has at least one nasal sound. Does the nasal character of these sounds spill over to the nearby vowels? Are the adjacent consonants distorted by nasality? Reread the following passage while you close the nostrils with your thumb and forefinger: "Let your speech always be gracious. . . . " There are no nasal sounds in these words. Your production of the sounds should not be materially altered even though you prohibit the operation of normal nasal resonation by closing off the nasal cavity. Read the rest of that sentence with the nostrils closed and discover what happens to *seasoned, may know, answer*, and *one*.

Listen to the quality of your voice. If you sense that you are possessed of a sound that isn't clear and pleasant to listen to, and if you are satisfied the fault is not pitch related, you probably are failing to use the resonating cavities properly as you produce your sounds. Admittedly, much of what we experience with resonance is addressed psychologically rather than physiologically: the result however may be a more pleasant-sounding voice, a clearer and better-functioning instrument.

**Articulation: The Production of Individual Speech Sounds**

The phonated, resonated sound is next acted upon by the articulators to be molded into intelligible speech sounds. The articulators are: 1. The lips; 2. The teeth; 3. The tongue; 4. The hard palate; 5. The soft palate; 6. The lower jaw. The articulators are used individually or in combination to alter the characteristics of the now-amplified and enriched tone. We have just discussed the nasal sounds. Each of these sounds [m, n, ŋ] we form

*The Communicative Basis of Preaching*

by forcing the sound into the nasal cavity by action of the articulators.

[m] is produced by stopping the sound's escape from the oral cavity with the two lips; as in *me*

[n] employs the tongue tip and the hard palate to force the sound into the nasal cavity; as in *no*

[ŋ] uses the back of the tongue and the soft palate to accomplish the same result; as in si*ng*

Vowels are essentially resonance phenomena but must be produced through the use of the articulators which alter the shape of the resonators—principally the oral cavity. Contrast, for example, the vowel sound in *me* [i] with the *ah* in father [a]. A chart[5] which graphically indicates the position of the tongue and the modification of the oral cavity for the production of each of the vowel sounds aids in the visualization of their formation:

High [i] *eat*                      [u] *boot*
       [ɪ] *it*                       [ʊ] *look*

Mid [e] *ch*a*os*       [ɜ˞] *bi*r*d*      [o] *o*b*ey*
      [ɛ] *met*       [ə] *sofa* [ɚ] *bette*r   [ɔ] *ou*g*ht*

Low [æ]*at*           [ʌ] c*u*t      [a] *a*r*t*
     Front              Central             Back

Diphthongs are combinations of vowels which form a single speech sound. They function as vowels.

[aɪ] *eye, I*
[aʊ] c*ow*
[ɔɪ] b*oy*
[eɪ] pl*ay*
[oʊ] t*oe*

The nasal sounds and the vowels are always voiced: That is, the vocal folds vibrate when the sounds are produced. Other sounds except the glides [j], [r], and [l] have voiceless and voiced counterparts:

plosive consonants

| | | |
|---|---|---|
| [p - b] | *p*ut - *b*ack | (formed with upper and lower lips) |
| [t - d] | *t*wo - *d*ogs | (formed with tongue tip and upper gum ridge) |
| [k - g] | *k*eep - *g*oing | (formed with tongue blade and hard palate) |

fricative consonants

| | | |
|---|---|---|
| [f - v] | *f*ix - *v*ex | (teeth and lower lip) |
| [θ - ð] | *th*in - *th*en | (note these vowels: [ɪ] and [e]) (tongue and upper teeth) |
| [s - z] | *s*o - *z*oo | (tongue tip and upper gum ridge) |
| [ʃ - ʒ] | *sh*e - mea*s*ure | (tongue, flattened, and palate) |
| [h] | *h*e | (breath only) |

affricative consonants

| | | |
|---|---|---|
| [tʃ - ʤ] | *ch*eap - *j*u*dg*e | ([ʃ] exploded through [t]; [ʒ] exploded through [d]) |

glides

| | | |
|---|---|---|
| [hw - w] | *wh*en - *w*in | (note these vowels: [ɛ] and [ɪ]) (lips) |

voiced glides

[j] *y*ou (tongue sides raised and palate)
[r] *r*un (tongues curved upward and upper gum ridge)
[l] *l*et (tongue touches upper gum ridge)

Articulation faults are difficult to detect without aid from a competent instructor or other knowledgeable person. You may carefully pronounce each of the key words listed above, then isolate the sound and produce it alone. In each case note the articulators indicated for the productions of the sound. Does your production correspond with these descriptions? Note any discrepancy to call to the attention of your instructor. Use a recording to check the clarity of each word and sound. Discuss with your instructor uncertainties you have, based upon careful listening to the recording. Ear training will aid you in identifying troublesome problem areas.

**Combining Speech Sounds into Words**

If *articulation* is the formation of individual speech sounds by action of the articulators, *pronunciation* is the combination of individual speech sounds in an acceptable sequence with proper stress to form words. Selection of sounds, their sequence, and degrees of stress are established by current usage indicated in standard sources such as dictionaries.

To improve one's pronunciation, an individual should become aware of probable problem areas. Pronunciation errors[6] may be grouped as follows:

omission—leaving out an essential sound from those which make up a word;

addition—adding sounds;

substitution—replacing one sound with another;

reversal of sounds—modifying the order of adjacent sounds (or at a distance);

restressing—a three-phase error which occurs when a stressed vowel is unstressed in connected speech, then restressed, altering the vowel (frequently from [a] to [ə] to [ʌ]);

voicing/unvoicing—changing the acceptable action of the vocal folds in the production of sounds;

spelling pronunciation—including sounds because spelling seems to require their presence.

Consider the following examples in each category. Can you add others from your awareness of problem pronunciations?

*omission*

| | | |
|---|---|---|
| su_prise for surprise | [sə'praɪz] | for [sɚ'praɪz] |
| Feb_uary for February | [fɛbjuerɪ] | for [fɛbruerɪ] |
| gover_ment for government | [gʌvɚmənt] | for [gʌvɚnmənt] |
| larges_ for largest | [lardʒɪs] | for [lardʒɪst] |
| win_er for winter | [wɪnɚ] | for [wɪntɚ] |
| cos_s for costs | [kɔsː] | for [kɔst] |
| chir*r*en for children | [tʃɪrːɪn] | for [tʃɪldrɪn] |
| hunnert for hundred | [hʌnɚt] | for [hʌndrɛd] |
| *s*atistics for statistics | [sə'tɪstɪks] | for [stə'tɪstɪks] |
| pacific for specific | [pəsɪfɪk] | for [spəsɪfɪk] |

*addition*

| | | |
|---|---|---|
| ath*a*lete for athlete | [æθəlit] | for [æθlit] |
| Illino*is* | [ɪlɪnɔɪz] | for [ɪlɪnɔɪ] also spelling pronunciation |
| often | [ɔftən] | for [ɔfən] spelling pronunciation |

## The Communicative Basis of Preaching

| twice | [twaɪst] | for [twaɪs] spelling pronunciation |
|---|---|---|
| grievous | [grivɪəs] | for [grivəs] |
| towards | [tə'wɔrdz] | for [tord] also addition and spelling pronunciation |

*substitution*

| height | [haɪt] | not [haɪθ] |
|---|---|---|
| reading | [ridɪŋ] | not [ridɪn] |
| brethren | [brɛðrɪn] | not [brʌðərɪn] also pronunciation by analogy to *brother* |
| any | [ɛnɪ] | not [ɪnɪ] |
| ten | [tɛn] | not [tɪn] |
| I | [aɪ] | not [a] |
| right | [raɪt] | not [rat] |
| egg | [ɛg] | not [eɪg] |
| better | [bɛtɚ] | not [bɛdɚ] also voicing |
| get | [gɛt] | not [gɪt] |
| oil | [ɔɪl] | not [ɔl] or [ɝl] |

*reversal of sounds*

| hundred | [hʌndrɪd] | not [hʌnɚt] also omission and unvoicing |
|---|---|---|
| ask | [æsk] | not [æks] |
| modern | [madɚn] | not [madrɪn] |
| perspiration | [pɝspərɛʃən] | not [prɛspərɛʃən] |
| Calvary | [kælvərɪ] | not [kævəlrɪ] |
| relevant | [rɛləvənt] | not [rɛvələnt] |
| prescription | [prɪ'skrɪpʃən] | not [pɚ'skrɪpʃən] |

*restressing*

| | | | |
|---|---|---|---|
| from | [fram] | unstressed to [frəm'hom] | restressed to [frʌm] |
| was | [waz] | unstressed to [wəz'rɛd] | restressed to [wʌz] |
| what | [hwat] | unstressed to [whət'kaɪnd] | restressed to [hwʌt] |
| of | [av] | unstressed to [əv'maɪn] | restressed to [ʌv] |

*voicing/unvoicing*

| | | | |
|---|---|---|---|
| Baptist | [bæptɪst] | not [bæbtɪst] | or [bæbdɪst] |
| killed | [kɪld] | not [kɪlt] | |
| notice | [notɪs] | not [nodɪs] | |
| water | [watɚ] | not [wadɚ] | or [wadə] |

*spelling pronunciation*

| | | | |
|---|---|---|---|
| [ɔftən] | for | [ɔfən] | often |
| [sɑlm] | for | [sɑm] | psalm |
| [ɪlɪnɔɪz] | for | [ɪlɪnɔɪ] | Illinois |
| [tʃæzəm] | for | [kæzəm] | chasm |
| [skɪzəm] | for | [sɪzəm] | schism |
| [melfæktɚ] | for | [mæləfæktɚ] | malefactor |
| [kamptrolɚ] | for | [kən'trolɚ] | comptroller |

A review of these categories of pronunciation error has doubtless brought other examples to mind. Ministers are among those who set pronunciation standards for the community. Careless habits must be addressed, therefore, so that one's effectiveness as a communicator will not be undermined. Communication will suffer if the pastor consistently makes pronunciation errors. He will be heard more than the message he has been given.

Consider the impact of these errors upon the assessment of the preacher's care in preparing his message:

| | | | |
|---|---|---|---|
| John the *Baptist* | [bæbtɪst] | for | [bæptɪst] |
| Holy *Spirit* | [spɪrt] | for | [spɪrɪt] |
| Holy *Ghost* | [gos] | for | [gost] |
| Jesus *Christ* | [kraɪsː] | for | [kraɪst] |
| Nazareth | [næzrəθ] | for | [næzərəθ] |
| Jerusalem | [ʤəruslɪm] | for | [ʤərusəlɪm] |
| Lord | [lard] | for | [lord] |

We have already cautioned the minister to be careful about placing too much stress on the first syllable of the name, Jesus [ʤizəs]. It should receive no more stress than the first syllable in David [devɪd]. Care should be taken as well to pronounce God with [a], as [gad], the [a] as in f*a*ther, r*o*d or c*o*t. Some preachers raise the vowel almost to [ɔ] as in [gɔd], G*aw*d. Others move the vowel forward toward [aɪ] so that it is pronounced somewhere nearer g*ui*de than God. If you have any reason to believe your pronunciation of the names of God and Jesus needs attention, by all means make some inquiry. Every servant should know the pronunciation of his master's name.

We are born into a language environment. Widening experiences continue processes of word assimilation begun in the home. Our vocabularies grow dramatically for a time, slow, and then almost stop developing. With our grasp of meanings comes our characteristic modes of saying words. Our reading vocabulary may outstrip our speaking one. In some contexts, we may not be comfortable trying new words. Like others whose speech is tied to the pursuit of their particular vocation, preachers need to harness words to the work they do.

Exactness of expression with precision in pronunciation are essential.

Repetition of a pronunciation error establishes habits difficult to break; difficult, but not impossible. These suggestions should prove helpful:

1. In your reading when you encounter a word whose meaning is obscure, check the pronunciation when you look up its meaning. Try saying the word aloud several times to fix its sounds and the meaning in mind.
2. Learn to recognize obvious errors in your pronunciation. All of us lapse into an occasional "git," but when we do, we should note the lapse and strive to overcome it just as we have successfully omitted "ain't" from grammatical usage in our sermons.
3. Always check the pronunciation of words, especially proper nouns, in the Scripture readings for public worship. Stumbling over King Ahasuerus's name may cause you to garble a familiar word such as Esther.
4. Ask your spouse or another friend to help you discover pronunciation problems. Habitual patterns of pronunciation are difficult to change. They sound fine to us. When we have identified a problem area, a friend can be helpful in listening for any lapse we may commit.
5. Do not develop an over-precise, pedantic mode of pronunciation. Remember that *art conceals itself*. Pronunciation contributes to intelligibility, not to the prominence and prestige of the preacher. For one to leave the service saying, "My, the preacher is articulate," may be less a compliment than,

"Today Christ became more real to me than ever before."

## Connected Speech: Sense in Sequence

We have discussed *stress* in connection with syllables in words. Our definition, the relative force or intensity with which a syllable is spoken, applies as well to patterns of stress in connected words. The sense of a sentence dictates the stress patterns which operate in connected speech. What happens when stress is arbitrarily arranged in the following:

1. *Ye* are the light of the world.
2. Ye *are* the light of the world.
3. Ye are *the* light of the world.
4. Ye are the *light* of the world.
5. Ye are the light *of* the world.
6. Ye are the light of *the* world.
7. Ye are the light of the *world*.

Only five and six seem contrived. Stress may identify the hearers of the message particularly (1), their significant role (4), their unique position (3), or their area of service (7).

Generally, nouns and verbs are among the most important words in connected speech. Adjectives move toward the nouns they modify and generally are less crucial to the sense of the sentence. Adverbs play a similar role for verbs. The indefinite articles, *a, an,* and the definite article, *the,* do not ordinarily receive stress. We find an exception, of course, in number 3 when the *exclusive* assignment to be light is acknowledged: "Ye are *the* light. . . ."

Persons for whom English is a second language, find

the stress patterns of our tongue difficult. For the most part, we have only to perceive the sense of a sentence to recognize where stress reasonably falls. Remember, when everything is stressed, nothing is. The over-precise, pedantic preacher will glory in "a" and "the," in conjunctions and prepositions, with the result that the real workhorses of our language, nouns and verbs, must be sought among words uniformly emphasized.

In the passage from John 10 in which Jesus characterized himself as the "good shepherd," note how meaning is expressed in nouns, pronouns, and verbs.

> Truly, truly I say to you, I am the door of the sheep. All who come before me are thieves and robbers; but the sheep did not heed them. I am the door, if any one enters by me, he will be saved, and will go in and out and find pasture. The thief comes only to steal and kill and destroy: I came that they may have life and have it abundantly. I am the good shepherd. The good shepherd lays down his life for the sheep.

Note that the adjective "good" moves us toward the concept "shepherd" and requires stress. The adverb "abundantly" describes how those who enter may *have* life. Again, the sense of the sentence requires that the adverb receive emphasis. Perhaps only three or four words in the passage require *unusual* stress: *door, am* (l. 4), *life, abundantly,* and *good shepherd* should be considered for particular stress. Mark with a second line the words you feel require heavy stress. Next, divide the passage into phrases, units of thought which hold together. Separate these with indications of pauses: slight /, medium // dramatic ///. Slight pauses accommodate our need to breathe and *may* correspond with the punctuation. A medium or moderate pause generally indicates a transition to another idea and follows the resolution of the preceding thought. A dramatic pause allows reflection upon what has been said or builds expectation for what is about to be said. After we have analyzed a text for reading, it would appear similar to the following:

> Lo!/I tell you a mystery.///We shall not all sleep,/but we shall all be changed,/in a moment,/in the twinkling of an eye,/at the last/trumpet.//For the trumpet will sound,/and the dead will be raised imperishable,/and we/shall be changed.//For this perishable nature must put on the imperishable and this mortal nature must put on immortality.//When the perishable puts on the imperishable, and the mortal puts on immortality,/then shall come to pass the saying that is written://
> "Death is swallowed up in victory."
> "O death,/where is thy victory?/
> O death,/where is thy sting?"/
> The sting of death is sin, and the power of sin is the law./But thanks be to God/who gives us the victory/ through our Lord Jesus Christ (1 Cor. 15:15-56).

The sense of the passages requires variety in *rate*. Since the first line unfolds a new idea, the rate should be *slow*. Perhaps a dramatic pause before "We shall not all sleep . . ." sets the readiness of the hearers to listen to the "mystery." A moderate rate seems indicated for the beginning of line two, but beginning with "in a moment . . ." the rate should be rapid. A moderate rate seems suited to the explanation that follows. The sentence which introduces the quotation repeats the previous idea and may be presented rapidly, building to "Death is swallowed up in victory." The final sentence should be spoken deliberately since it concludes the passage and ties the change to imperishable, to immortality, to the victory secure through our Lord Jesus Christ. Read the passage through several times and mark the appropriate rate of speech: slow (sl.), moderate (md.), and rapid (rp.), where they seem called for. Such aids should help the preacher *in practice* to cultivate sensitivity to the presentation of ideas. Once analysis and practice are concluded, the preacher should return to the text and allow the Holy Spirit to use that preparation as he enlivens the words of Scripture, making them imperishable, immortal.

## Ministerial Tone: Please Don't Play that Tune Again!

Hardly a contemporary textbook on preaching has omitted mention of ministerial tone or tune in discussions of vocal delivery. No one is precise in defining the phenomenon all of us recognize: We know it when we hear it; but like a legitimate Southern accent, the ministerial tune is difficult to reproduce and impossible to describe definitively.

The principal feature of ministerial tune is patterned inflectional variation. It may be built on a series of ascending patterns with each sequence in turn beginning on a slightly higher pitch and moving upward before the phrase returns to the next beginning, slightly higher pitch. When the ascending patterns reach the point of highest intensity, dictated more by the limits of the voice than by the sense of the communication, the preacher drops down to pitch level to begin the sequence again.

## The Communicative Basis of Preaching

A series of descending inflectional patterns is just as likely and just as tied to the sense of what is being said. Or the preacher may use a circumflex pattern with variations up and down within phrases. You may experiment with any composition to experience the rising, falling, or circumflex patterns. To avoid sacrilege, use a portion of the funeral oration of Antony in *Julius Caesar*.

> Friends, Romans, countrymen, lend me your ears;
> I come to bury Caesar, not to praise him.
> The evil that men do lives after them;
> The good is oft interred with their bones;
> So let it be with Caesar (Act III, Sc. 2).

Ministerial tone has rhythmic elements as well as inflectional ones. The pattern is akin to the chant: Stress does not necessarily follow meaning but becomes a part of the pattern. Detractors of clergymen have mastered this "preachy" mode of address. The fact that we readily recognize this stereotypical representation of preaching adds to our discomfort.

Our goal should be to speak *directly, forcefully, vigorously,* but *conversationally*. Admittedly a sermon is not a one-on-one conversation. It partakes of the form, however, of personal witness, of testimony, of individual narrative, of the minister's response to the gospel. As personal communication, it is *conversational*. In keeping with the transforming power of the gospel, it must be *direct, forceful,* and *vigorous*. To be sure, preaching must not be perceived as insincere but as genuine. The former may be the response to the preaching style of presentation we call ministerial tone.

The latter response should be facilitated by conversational address.

**The Body in Action: Movement and Gesture**

We have indicated already that the message consists both of what the ear hears and the eye sees. We have noted that with verbal communication we must eliminate any signal to the hearers that may be interpreted negatively. Nonverbal communication has the capability of reinforcing or undermining our intended message.

Consider the question, When does the sermon begin? The responses could include, after the anthem, or when the text is read, or when the minister begins to speak. Actually, the preacher begins to send signals which will affect the hearers' readiness to listen and respond long before he approaches the pulpit with sermon notes and Bible in hand. As soon as we identify the minister as the one we shall hear, we begin to read his nonverbal messages, consciously or unconsciously.

The preacher's dress and grooming tell us something of his personal attitudes and habits. If he is inattentive during the service, evidenced by his gazing into space, drumming his fingers on the arms of his chair, or shuffling through his Bible or sermon notes, he tells us he has little regard for worship apart from the sermon. He sends a similar signal by a lack of participation in singing or other portions of the order of service he does not lead. Even though he may engage in deep, public meditation, he speaks nonverbally of his attitudes about the importance of what he rejects in favor of his contemplation during the service.

The minister's role as leader in worship extends

beyond these particular assignments he has accepted in the order of worship. He, along with all those before the congregation (those on the platform or in the choir), should challenge the others who worship by their examples of attention, reverence, participation, and enjoyment of the experience. Those who lead in worship should mirror the intended response among the congregation to encourage the worshipers' attention, reverence, participation, and enjoyment.

While we have no wish to be prescriptive in matters of taste, we would encourage the minister to carefully consider his nonverbal signals. Among characteristics and attributes the minister should review are the following.

1. Conservative dress in the pulpit and appropriate clothing everywhere. If the choice of suit, sports coat and slacks, tie, or shoes calls attention to the minister, he may be inappropriately dressed. Again, a coat and tie for a picnic sends interesting signals about the preacher's common sense.
2. Good grooming.
3. Involvement and participation in all components of the service of worship.
4. Good posture when sitting and standing.

**Energy in Presentation**

The minister must be involved physically in his preaching. We give evidence of this involvement through directness and forcefulness in our delivery. We communicate directness through eye contact, vocal energy, and physical projection of our total identification with our message. The extent of our identification is revealed as much by muscle tension and relaxation as by overt movement. While we may move in the direction of the congregation to express an intense desire to be understood or to encourage their participation as active listeners in a particularly important part of our message, throughout our presentations we shall encourage their *empathic involvement* as they become tense and relax in response to our action.

Directness of eye contact aids in hearer response. Care should be taken, however, that eye contact enhance the impact of the message and not diminish it. Some elements of a message may actually suffer from direct eye contact, particularly a closed conversation in a narrative, address to someone not present, or statements directed to God. Generally, however, explanations, directions, appeals, first-person narratives, and challenges require eye contact for maximal impact.

**Gestures as an Extension of Speaker Involvement**

Gestures may be broadly defined as any movement designed to reinforce the statement of an idea. Movement of the body as a whole as previously described represents gesture as does the lifting of an eyebrow. Movement, then, of the body, the arms, the hands, the fingers, and the face may accompany the expression of a thought and be interpreted as a gesture.

Gestures should be extensions of the speaker's involvement in his message. Since they emanate from the presentation of thought to reinforce its expression, gestures should be *purposive*, not random. Again the *timing* of gestures is crucial to their effect. An off-timed gesture we find amusing. Gestures should be *appropri-*

ate. A formal or solemn occasion generally gives rise to fewer gestures than an informal one. Broad gestures in a small space look awkward; subtle gestures in a large auditorium will be missed. Gestures should be *clear;* they should not confuse or contribute to ambiguity occasioned by the speaker's inadvertent use of a *conventional* gesture.

Some gestures, indeed, are *conventional.* A numbering gesture we recognize readily. The clenched fist suggests hostility; the raised hands palms out with a gentle movement up and down encourages peaceful response or settling down. Bowed heads indicate prayer. To use a clenched fist to represent our Lord's compassion toward the multitude could create ambiguity.

*Descriptive* gestures are useful for giving instructions or aiding the mind's eye to perceive the size, shape, or other features of an object. A veteran chapel speaker/observer suggested that college students were often more attentive in campus worship services than we realize. He said, "Watch what happens when the preacher says, 'It was about so high.' Heads will immediately rise as eyes seek to interpret the gesture." Like all good movement, descriptive gestures aid the language of the message, afford variety, and stimulate attention.

The preacher should be animated but not compulsively active. The key to the use of good gestures is the extent to which they enhance the effectiveness of the message. Practice of sermon delivery before a mirror may aid the preacher in developing gestures. Care should be taken, however, that practiced gestures appear *spontaneous* and *natural.* Otherwise, they should be omitted.

## Integrated Verbal and Nonverbal Communication

Throughout this chapter we have emphasized the importance of both verbal and nonverbal communication. While, for convenience, we have divided our consideration of these two types of signals, in reality they are (in the live preaching situation) indivisible. The absence of physical involvement coupled with poor articulation sends a clear message to the hearer about the preacher's competence and, indeed, his estimate of the importance of his task. An animated, articulate preacher with something significant to say will always find hearers ready to respond and actively listen.

We can facilitate the integration of these communication behaviors by understanding and employing *projection* when we preach. Adequate loudness is a dimension of this phenomenon. Thus, projection is related to physical aspects of voice production. Careful articulation aids projection. But integral to how we *project* is the psychological intention to be heard and to evoke response. It is a matter of directing our communication to specific hearers. Thus, we project to the last row and all can hear and understand. We project to representative target groups within a large audience, and everyone feels we are talking to him. While the presence of a public address system for amplifying the voice lessens the need for loudness, the preacher must nevertheless project in order to be heard and understood. Projecting is tied to the desire to get the message across. A failure to project is a negative signal indicating the absence of this desire.

The preacher should always be motivated to communicate with intensity the message he has prepared. He looks for response. He appreciates the compelling significance of his task. To decide between having something to say and saying it well is to afford an unfortunate choice. Both are worthy. One enhances the other.

Personal commitment cannot be a matter of the intellect alone. We express faith in whole persons. In the language of the Shema, Jesus reminded us that we must love the Lord, our God, with all our heart, soul, mind, and strength. Our emotions, religious responsiveness, intellect, and fervor must all be harnessed to the expression of our love of God. Expression of that love in preaching must be holistic as well: Verbally and nonverbally alike we bear witness to the truth we have encountered in Jesus Christ. And the Holy Spirit enlivens the Word of truth we communicate.

### Think on These Things

1. Identify a contemporary pulpit figure you consider to be a good model for the young minister. Describe the attributes you feel so qualify him.
2. Listen to tape recordings of preaching. How many faults of voice production do you hear? Are some problems encountered more frequently than others?
3. Consult voice and articulation texts to discover exercises which are suggested to address voice problems. Develop a card file of such exercises. Note those which seem of particular value to you.
4. Using a recent translation of Scripture, identify a passage which will aid you in addressing voice and

articulation problems. Type the passage. Mark it for phrases and stress. Practice reading it until it is almost committed to memory. Check the pronunciation of any unusual names and words. Capture the sense of the passage in your emotional and rational response to the language.
5. Develop a list of mispronounced words you hear in a given week. What categories of error seem to be recurrent? What words others pronounce incorrectly do you recognize in your pronunciation?
6. Listen to connected address for verbal stalls: "you know," "uhhh," "it seems to me that," and the like. Tabulate your findings.
7. Apply the dictum, "Art conceals itself," to the preacher as communicator.
8. Listen to recorded sermons to find a good example of ministerial tone or tune. Try to describe its patterned inflectional characteristics. Can you diagram them?
9. Attend a service of worship. Analyze the nonverbal signals from the ministers you receive as a participant in the service.
10. Describe conventional gestures we are apt to encounter in worship.

### Suggested Reading

Baird, A. Craig; Knower, Franklin H.; Becker, Samuel L. *General Speech Communication.* New York: McGraw-Hill Book Company, 1971.

Bartow, Charles L. *The Preaching Moment.* Nashville: Abingdon Press, 1980.

Chartier, Myron R. *Preaching as Communication.* Nashville: Abingdon Press, 1981.
Fairbanks, Grant. *Voice and Articulation Drillbook.* New York: Harper & Row, 1937.
Fasol, Al. *A Guide to Self-Improvement in Sermon Delivery.* Grand Rapids, Michigan: Baker Book House, 1983.
Fisher, Hilda B. *Improving Voice and Articulation.* Boston: Houghton Mifflin Company, 1966.
Hanley, Theodore D. and Wayne L. Thurman. *Developing Vocal Skills.* New York: Holt, Rinehart and Winston, 1962.
Lucas, Stephen, E. *The Art of Public Speaking.* New York: Random House, 1983.
Rogge, Edward and James C. Ching. *Advanced Public Speaking.* New York: Holt, Rinehart and Winston, Inc., 1966.

### Notes

1. Clyde E. Fant, *Preaching for Today* (New York: Harper and Row, 1975), p. 145 ff.

2. Ralph P. Martin, *The Worship of God* (Grand Rapids: William B. Eerdmans, 1982), p. 101 ff., includes an interesting discussion of the place of the sermon in worship.

3. Much of the material included in this chapter comes from teaching of courses in voice and articulation. The author acknowledges his debt to many textbooks in the field employed from time to time, some of which are included in the suggested reading list.

4. To indicate individual speech sounds, we shall employ the symbols of the International Phonetic Alphabet.

5. The sounds included herein are those used in general American speech. Other dialects require additional sounds.

6. For a comprehensive discussion of pronunciation error, see Claude Merton Wise, *Applied Phonetics* (Englewood Cliffs, N.J.: Prentiss-Hall, Inc., 1957), p. 182 ff.

# Index

Abimelech 116
Abraham 119, 152, 155, 158, 182, 183
Absalom 161
abstraction 181, 185, 186
Achtemeier, Elizabeth 201
action 77; call to 97, 170
Acts, Book of 9
Adam 154
address, conversational 241-242
adjectives, use of 191-192, 237-238
adverbs, use of 191-192, 237-238
affirmation of sermon 88-90, 94, 109-110, 111, 115, 167
*agape* 74, 78
ark of the covenant 81
allegiance to God 166
alliteration 205-207
allusion 190
ambiguity 185, 245
Ambrose 12
Amos 5, 135
anachronism 195
analysis of sermons 192
Ananias 9
anaphora 200, 202
antimetabole 200, 202
apologists 12
apostle 7-9
apostles 169
apostrophe 200

appeals, motivational 64-69; principles for use of 70
application 110, 158, 171, 174
Aquinas, Thomas 13
argument 69, 79; power of 77-81, 87; use of 73-74
arrangement of supporting material 91
art of preaching 217
art, verbal 178
articles, definite 237; indefinite 237
articulation 228-231; faults of 231
articulators 228-229
Asia Minor 11
assonance 206
Athenians 37
attention 47, 53
attitude of the hearers 47, 57; of the minister 59
audience, characteristics of 55-56
Augustine 12, 129
authority, of God's Word 14; biblical 141, 163

Baal, prophets of 166
babbler 37
Babylon 5
balance in sermons 175
baptism 7, 43, 169
Barnabas 10, 30

# Index

Basil the Great 12
Beatitudes 157
beauty 46; in expression 179
behavior, human 103
belief 169
believer 44
believers, fellowship of 42
Bible 103, 110, 112, 122, 135, 154-155; as authority 94-96; content of 16; study of 61, 104, 105, 107; translations of 141; world of 102, 109
biblical theology 3
biographies, biography 129, 139, 158
bond—rapport 38
breathing for speech 220-222, 224
brevity 173
Broadus, John A. 190, 201
Bunyan, John 120, 129
Buttrick, George 85

Caesarea 9
call to ministry 27, 29, 30, 40; to preach 28
Calvin, John 14
canon 12, 94, 105
caring, climate of 63
casual argument as support 85-86
celebration in worship 20
Cephas 182
character 36, 110
characteristics of listeners 51-63
Cheevers, John 139
children 180-183
children of God 34
children of Israel 182
choice, freedom of 154
Christ 8, 9, 10, 15, 16, 17, 18, 19, 20, 21, 32, 35, 52, 59, 70, 120; lordship of 136, 162; love of 35; preaching of 51; return of 160
Christian 25, 28, 34, 185

Christianity 11, 34; spread of 11
Christians 9, 11, 20, 33
Christmas 106
chronology 82
Chrysostom 12
church 10, 11, 12, 13, 14, 15, 16, 17, 155, 160; body of Christ 19, 84; Eastern Orthodox 12; gathered 17, 42; local 25; New Testament 30; Roman 12, 14; spread of 11
churches, rural 62
clarity 46, 47, 114, 118, 173, 179, 184, 193
classics of devotion 129
Claypool, John 163-164
Clement of Alexandria 12
clergy 13
Clinard, Gordon 104
Clowney, Edmund 6
comforter 32
commentaries 109, 114, 115
commentary, running 149
Commission, Great 187, 205, 206
commitment 18, 26, 27, 30, 35, 49, 93, 120
committee, pastoral search 56
communication 35, 39, 40; cycle 44-45, 50; environment 46; nonverbal 242, 243; oral 183; religious 179, 219
Communications, Model 44; process 44, 48
communicative act 45
communicator 16
community 120
comparison 118, 169, 199; as support 83-84
compassion 103
competency (in ministry) 29
competing signals in worship 47
comprehension (of message) 44, 49, 80
compulsion, inner 36

concentration 54
conclusion 78; of sermon 111, 173
confession 7, 169
confession of faith 18
confidence 25; in preaching 118
conflict, resolution of 97, 167
confrontation 166
congregation(al) 15, 25, 31, 43, 45, 49, 52, 56-58, 108, 110, 121, 131
conjunctions, use of 238
consonants 230; affricative 230; fricative 223, 230; plosives 230
contacts, pastoral 105
contemplative life 85
content (of sermon) 46
context of ministry 132; of proclamation 131-137
contrast 118, 169; as support 84
controversy 63
conversion of Saul 9-10, 155, 159
conviction(s) 62, 97, 136
convince 77, 97
correspondence, theory of 44
corruption 135
counseling 38, 143
counselor(s) 36, 39, 161
courage 121
covenant, ark of 6
Crammer, Thomas 14
creation 2, 154, 165
creativity 156
Creator 102
credibility 79
crises of life 161
crisis 110, 162
cross 17
cross-references 113-114
crucifixion 17
culture 29, 137, 163; knowledge of 137
Cyprian 12

Damascus 10

Dargan, E.C. 150
David 120, 156, 161
death 161
Decalogue 149
decision 18, 64
declaration 5, 38
deduction 79
deductive, sermon model 88; preaching 90; beginning 171
definitions as support 82-83
Demas 159
description, as support 81-82; skills of 193-195
devotion 166
devotional 128, 129, 130, 131, 141, 154
dialectic (in worship) 71-72, 73
dialogue in worship 71, 73; with text 128
diaphragm 220-222
diaphragmatic breathing 220-222
didactic sermon 96
diphthongs 229
disciples, preaching of 52
discipleship 72-73
discipline 130, 133-134
discovery, serendipitous 104; joy of 117; of meaning 116
discussion groups 135
doctrine 116
doers of Word 52
Dominic 13

ear training 231
Easter 106
echo 136
Eden, Garden of 154
edification 52
education 53
effectiveness of preacher 39; in preaching 64, 73-74; in ministry 218
Eleazar 158
Elijah 166

# Index

Eliot, T. S. 138
emotional proof 64-65, 69
empathic involvement 244
energy in sermon presentation 243-244
Esau 158
eschatology 160, 167-168
eternity 21
ethical appeal 64
ethical proof 64
ethos 58, 60, 69
Eucharist 14
evaluation 39
Eve 154
event, communicative 178
events, current 133-135
evidence, use of 80-101; tests of 86-87
evil 5
exaltation of Jesus 10
exegesis 115
Exile, Babylonian 7, 149
Exodus, Book of 155
explanation in sermons 81
exposition, biblical 96, 149-152
expression 44, 46, 113, 178; concrete 185; exactness in 190-191; imagistic 198; in writing 198; joy of 145; power of 37-38; verbal 200, 225; written 183-184
eye contact 47, 243, 244
eyewitnesses 11
Ezekiel 5
Ezra 7

faith 25-28, 31, 32, 34, 40, 42-43, 48, 51, 60, 79, 84, 93, 113, 120, 121, 166; as support 91-93l commonality in (of) 70, 92; community of 26, 29-30, 42; contents of 27, 31; life of 35
family (of minister) 129
Father 8, 9, 32, 34, 103; love of 186
fatigue 54

fears 132
feedback 38, 45, 49, 50
fellowship 15, 27
festivals 106
figures of speech 201-204
Fisher, Wallace 27, 29, 30
flesh 21
flock 153
foretellers 6
forgiveness 9, 10, 167
Fourth Lateran Council 13
Foxe 129
Francis of Assisi 13, 78
future 6

genre 152-159
gestures 244-245
Gethsemane 107
Gideon 156
gifts for ministry 30
Gilead, balm of 36
God 5, 15, 17, 19, 20, 25, 32, 59, 70, 83, 153, 182, 183; grief of 5; heart of 5; love of 117; majesty of 122; name of 130; power of 10, 38; will of 5, 129; Word 14; worship of 42; wrath of 5, 8, 117
good news 10, 25
gospel 10, 15, 27, 35, 38, 40, 52, 70, 143-144; demands of 33-35
grace 52, 83
grace, Word of 42, 43, 60
grammar 112; errors in 214
grammars 141
Greek language 12, 112
Gregory of Nazianzus 12
grief 161
group response, dynamics of 57
growth, Christian 25, 26, 27, 31

health, spiritual 49-50
hearer(s) 46, 47, 48, 50, 51, 52, 111, 140, 141-142, 242
hearing 51, 52, 93

heart 18, 27, 145
Hebrew language 112
Hebrews, Epistle to the (Book of) 119, 158
Hellenism 12
herald 3, 25
hermeneutics 112
history 120, 132; of church 120
hoarseness (hoarse) 220, 224, 226
Holland, T. Dewitte 13
holy 27, 34
Holy Ghost 9; Spirit 17, 20, 32, 44, 46, 47-48, 59, 79, 93, 95-96, 160, 162, 216, 240, 247
home, sermon on 165
homiletics, definition 114
homily 149-152
homogeneity 55-57
homonyms 190
honesty 37
hope 6, 21, 132
Hopkins, Gerard Manly 138
Hosea 5
humility 110
humor 60
hunger 133
Huxley 132
hymns 199-200
hyperbole 202
hypernasality 227
hypocrisy 144
hyponasality 227
hyptyposis 203

idea, sermon 45, 126, 130; growth of 108, 126-127
ideas, acceptance of 64-65; perception of 64-65; presentation of 64, 240; retention of 104; maturity of 126-127
ideational, defined 126
identity 36, 182, 185-186
idioms 199
illusion 190

illustration 49, 81, 82, 118-119, 139; recording 122; sources of 119; use of 122-123
image, minister's 28-29
imagery 196-198
images 118; multi-sensory 196-198
imagination 156
impact of message 47-49
incarnation 17
inductive beginning 170-171
inductive preaching 90-91
inferences, nature of 77-80
inflation, verbal 20
information 20, 31, 32, 35, 77-78, 81, 132, 139, 188; gaining of 53
insensitivity 36
insights 145
inspiration 117, 129
instruction 102-103
integrated communication behavior 246-247
integrity 70, 73-74, 136; in ministry 29, 34-35; reciprocal 70, 74
intelligence of minister 58
intent of sermon 111
intention 78, 111-112, 190-191, 194
intentionality 46, 194
interest 53, 158
interpretation 48, 81, 85, 96, 112-118, 130, 148, 150; components of 112-118; history of 31
interpreter 16, 74, 110
introduction, purposes of 172
Issac 158, 182, 183
Isaiah; Book of 5, 6
Israel 5, 166, 182
Israelites 34
invitation 42-43, 111, 169, 174
involvement, empathic 244
Jabusch, Willard F. 26, 34
Jacob 158, 182, 183
jailer, Philippian 169

# Index

James 51-52
Jeremiah 2-3, 5, 34
Jerusalem 5, 9, 103
Jesus 7, 8, 10, 29, 32, 52, 60, 72, 84, 119, 137, 152, 153, 155, 157, 169, 198, 238; Christ 25, 29, 155; as Lord 72; life and ministry 155; as teacher 200
John, the apostle 9; Epistles of 158; Gospel of 210
John the Baptist 7-8, 10, 196, 198
Joseph 156, 158
Jotham 116
judgment(s) 5, 34, 135, 136
Judson, Adoniram (and Ann) 78, 120
justice 34, 70, 135
justification by faith 152

kerygma 10, 170
kingdom of heaven 84, 160
kings 6
knowledge 31-33, 138, 187
Knox, John 14

Laban 158
Lamb of God 8
larynx 219, 223, 224
language 138, 179, 182, 183, 199; colorful 199; common 48; development of 209; effect of 204; environment 181, 235; of faith 200; figurative 116, 199-204; imagistic 154, 196, 198; intelligible 207-208; Jesus' use of 200; non-talking 207; pictorial 201; sound of 204-208; symbolic 181, 182, 183; use of 203-204
Law 7, 149
Lazarus 103
leadership, divine 107-108
Leah 158
learner 26-27
learning 37

*lectio coutinua* 138
lectionary 106-107
lexicon 113, 115, 141
life 17, 21, 25, 36, 137
life-style modification 49
light 2, 21
listener 17, 21, 65, 139, 140, 141, 142; characteristics of 51-63; motives 64-65; response 65
listening 51, 52-63, 143; objectives 53; personal factors in 54; sermonic 143-144; setting factors in 54-55; skills 55; speaker factors in 54; subject factors in 54
listening behavior 43, 54-55
literary expression 116
literature 109, 139; Old Testament 155, 156
liturgy 13, 14
*Logos* 93
Lord 8, 25, 29, 59, 153
Lord's Supper 43
love 108, 156; of Christ 52; Christian 26; of God 83
Luther, Martin 14
man 40
manipulative strategies 73
manipulator 73
mannerisms 113
manuscript 33, 192, 209
Mark 8
Martha 196
Martyr, Justin 12
martyrdom 159
Mary 196
Mass 14
Matthew 169
maturation 108
maturity 27, 43, 49, 108; theological 181
meaning 83; comprehension of 113; discovery of (the) 114, 116; and language 180-183
media, nonprint 134

meditation 128, 130
memory 194, 209
Merton, Thomas 85
message 3, 15, 39, 45, 47, 48-50, 137, 213, 242; apprehend 48; Christian 20; claim of 47; content of 39, 191; continuity of 123; decoding 44, 45, 48-49; encoding 44, 45, 46, 48-49; environment 46; modification 49, 50; of the Bible 112; reception 50; reinforcement 50, 242, 244-245; response to 57; source 47, 50; transmission 44, 46-47, 48-49, 50; unity of 123; Word as 2-4
messenger 39, 122
Messiah 6, 8
metaphors 83, 181, 199-204
metonymy 200, 203
Micah 5
mind 27, 32, 130
minister(s) 4, 26, 27, 29, 31, 32, 35, 45, 55, 121; education of 58-59; example of morality 58; family of 59; as person 29
ministerial tone 240-242
ministry 8, 9, 28, 29, 30, 39, 50; preaching 50; prophetic 136
missions 188
models of preaching 216-218
monologue, dramatic 156
Moon, Lottie 120
morality 8
Moses 182, 195
motives 39
movement in sermons 172-173
music 19

name as identity 182, 183, 185-186
narration, as support 82
narrative(s), biblical 155, 180; Old Testament 155; preaching 155; sermon 154-156, 164, 174
nasality 227-228

nature of congregational response 63-70
nature, human 103
Naylor, Rebekah 120
needs, life 48
new birth 36
new hermeneutic 128
New Testament 16, 30
newsmagazine 134, 139
newspaper 134, 139
Nicodemus 71, 152, 169
Noah 119; ark of 84
noise 47
nouns 237-238; use of 191-193
nourishment of soul 128
novelist 139
novels 139

object lesson 165
objectives for preaching 96-99; sermon 111-112
observation 102; powers of 195
observer, preacher as 103
O'Connor, Flannery 139
Old Testament 29, 34
orator 40
order of service 64
ordinances 43
ordination 30
Origen 12
oxymoron 203

parable 111, 116, 160, 200
paradox 202
parallelism 207
Passover 81, 196
pastor(s) 7, 26, 27, 28, 29, 30-31, 143
pastorate 28
pathos 69
Paul 2, 3, 4, 9, 18, 29, 30, 31, 35, 37, 52, 65, 81, 119, 136, 156, 158, 159, 162, 188-189, 195
pauses 238-239

# Index

people 108, 143; involvement with 35-37; needs of 102-103
Pentecost, day of 9, 11, 16, 18, 149
personification 199, 201, 202
persuade 97
persuasion 62, 80
Peter 9, 10, 16, 136, 156
Pharisee 110
Philip 159
Philippi 195
Phoebe 159
phonation 219-220; faults of 224-226
piety 34-35
pitch 224, 225, 226
plan for preaching 105, 107, 127; of the sermon 99-100, 131
poetry, Hebrew 158
poets 138
power, creative 2
praise 20, 42, 43, 225
prayer 19, 27, 42, 43, 44, 46, 63, 85, 107, 110, 112, 128, 129, 137, 144
preach 1, 3, 4, 8, 9, 28, 34; verbs meaning 3-4
preacher(s) 1, 3, 15, 16, 17, 25, 26, 29, 32, 33, 34, 36, 37, 39, 44, 46, 47, 48, 51, 52, 57, 58, 85, 103, 110, 112, 131, 132, 143; as communicator 213-214; as listener 143; as theologian 16, 142; motivation of 73-74
preaching 1, 2, 3, 4, 15, 16, 17, 18, 19, 20, 25, 33, 40, 42, 43, 44, 46, 51, 52, 107, 110, 155, 178; as event 17; as oral medium 178; as verbal art 178; biblical 155; confessional 163-164; context for 215-216; definition 1-11; enrichment of 139, 140-142; history of 11-15; language of 179; memorable 148; mystery of 17; New Testament 7-11, 15, 17; Old Testament 4-7, 15; pastoral 39; power of 13; reformation 14-15; relevance of 20-21; television 217; theological significance of 15-18; theology of 19, 180
preparation for preaching 33; of sermon 61
priest(s) 6, 7, 31, 149
priesthood of believer 72
proclaim 3, 15, 16, 21, 145, 213
proclaimer 20
proclamation 1, 11, 12, 13, 16, 19, 21, 25, 35, 40, 43, 62, 71, 111, 130, 215; in worship 43
prodigal, story of 156, 172, 174, 186
progression in sermons 172-173
projection 246
pronunciation 214, 215, 231-237; errors in 232, 234, 236; standards 234
proof, logical 69, 70, 77
proof-texting 74, 95
prophecy 8
prophet(s) 2, 3, 5, 6, 7, 8, 9, 31; false 34; Old Testament 149
Protestantism 15
Proverbs 157
providence of God 6
psalmist 130, 153
pulpit 17, 39, 47, 52; behavior 214-216; ministries 217; power of 13; skill 216
punctuation 239
purpose(s) in preaching 97-98, 110, 164-165; of sermon 62, 63, 98-99, 110-111

Quintilian 40

rabbi 149
rapport 59-60
rate, variety in 239-240
Read, David H. C. 52
reading 52; plan for 137-140, 142; program of 120
reality 183, 185, 195

reason, use of 79-80, 93; and faith 93
reasoning 167
Rebecca 158
recall 148
reception 70
reconciler 63
reconciliation 63
redemption 3, 155; message of 135, 136; mystery of 117
reflection 77, 109, 128, 130, 131, 144
Reformation 13, 14, 15
reinforcement, reciprocal 63
relating, skills in 35-40
relevance 135, 200
repentance 5, 7, 9, 10, 136, 169
repetition 192, 205, 206
research 114
resonance 226-228; faults in 227
resonation 226
resonators 229
response 53; corporate 64; nature of 63-70; to preaching 38-39, 49, 63, 144; to sermon 111; in worship 43
restressing of sounds 232, 234
resurrection 10, 17, 20, 83, 155, 170
Reuben 158
revelation 3, 10; contents of 183; in language 181-182
reversal of sounds 231, 233
revival 62
rhetoric 4, 7, 12; Greek 7, 149; Roman 149
rhetorician 40
rhythmic elements in speaking 241
righteousness 70, 135, 137, 144
Roman Empire 12
Rome 12, 14

sacraments 12, 14, 15
salvation 32, 34, 38, 155, 169, 170; doctrine of 159
salvation history 10

Samaritan, the 186
Samson 156
Sarah 158
Savonarola, Girolamo 14
scholarship 141
scribes 7
Scripture(s) 17, 19, 21, 31, 37, 38, 44, 45, 49, 61, 102, 103, 163; exposition of 150-152; Old Testament 149; reading of 19; study of 152; as support 94-96; view of 19
Scudder, Ida 120
self-worth 36
sense; auditory 196; gustatory 196; kinesthetic 196; olfactory 196; thermal 196
sensitivity 126; cultivation of 127; spiritual 102
sermon(s) 3, 4, 9, 10, 14, 15, 16, 17, 33, 43, 61, 62, 104, 127, 143, 178; biographical 158; body 172-173; building the 13; children's 180; confessional 163-164; construction of 102; content 49, 160; to convince 167; development 107, 108, 138; devotional 153-154; didactic 157-158; doctrinal 159-160, 167; ethical 162-163; evangelistic 168-169; expository 150-152; form of 12, 13, 152-153; ideas 102-105, 110; inductive model of 89; to inform 164; intent 110-112, 173; life-situation 160-161; as living word 20; as message heard 219; New Testament 149; Old Testament 149; one point 157; on the Mount 157; organization of 148, 174-175; to persuade 168; plan 99-100; preparation of 45, 107, 112, 127; problem-solution 162-163; purpose of 62, 174; response 63-70; to stimulate 166; structure 148-

# Index

187; subject 107, 111; support 63; texts 105-107, 110, 148, 150-151; theological basis of 4; therapeutic 162; in worship 216
servant 29
service 35
seventy, the 18, 166
Shema 93, 247
shepherd 26, 153, 238
signals in communication 38-39, 48, 242; nonverbal 44, 46, 48, 53, 71; verbal 44, 46, 47, 48, 64, 71
Silas 195
similes 83, 199, 202
Simon Peter 136, 149, 182
simplification 84
sin 7, 8, 136, 154; awareness of 169; effects of 154
sincerity 110
skills, communicative 37, 38, 46, 50; evaluative 39; listening 48, 50, 52-53; pulpit 216; receptive 38-39; speaking 216; verbal 37, 38
slave 29
social issues 57
society 129, 135
Son 20
Song of Solomon 120
sounds 228-231; substitution of 231, 233
speak 33
speaking 52; public 3-4
specific aspects of sermon 88-91, 94
specific objective 174
specificity 186-189; resistance to 189
speech 2, 37
spelling pronunciation 232, 234
spirit 37; judgmental 39
Spirit 16, 17, 21, 25, 33, 52, 102, 108, 127, 171; guidance of 117; leadership of 117, 130; power of 210; presence of 117; role in preaching 180; as teacher 117; voice of 144

spiritual dimension of preaching 48, 127-131
Spurgeon, Charles Haddon 178
Stanfield, Vernon L. 201
statistics as support 84
Stephen 149, 159
Stevens, Wallace 138
stewardship 81, 97
stimulate 96-97, 154
story 82, 118; biblical 154-155; short 140
strategies for listening 55
Stratman, Gary 39
stress in words 237-238; patterns of 237, 241
stridency 224, 227
study 28; aids 141; biblical 140-142, 144; systematic plan of 116; theological 140-142, 144
style 113, 139, 140, 178, 179, 190, 192, 210; development of 209; extemporaneous 209; oral 208-210; spoken 192
success 33
Sunday School 27
support, effect of 87; forms of 80
supporting material 90, 139
symbol 81
symbolic actions 5, 43
symbolism 181, 182
synagogue 7, 26, 149
synonyms 190
Synoptic Gospels 113

tactile faculty 196
talents 39
teacher 31, 32
teaching 27, 80
teaching ministry 6
Temple 7, 9, 110, 135
temptation 8, 27, 34, 162
tension 220, 227
Tertullian 12
testimony 121; of Scripture 168-169; as support 85

text(s)  48, 51, 61, 94, 127, 131; multiple passage 159; selection of 105, 107, 110-111; validity of 77
Thanksgiving 106
theme 116
theologian 142
theology 3, 16, 31, 113, 142; biblical 144, 155; New Testament 142; Old Testament 142; systematic 117, 142
Thessalonica 136
Timothy 10, 158
tithe 81
tone 225, 226; amplified 228
topics 116, 159; of sermons 60, 97, 98, 107-109, 110
*torah* 6
tradition 31; liturgical 106; Protestant 42; Reformed 19
transition sentences 172, 173; in speaking 239
treasure 32, 145
trends, religious 136
trust 84
truth 20, 32, 70, 93, 144, 152, 171, 200, 247; of God 59; spoken 52

Underhill Evelyn 42
understanding 108
unity in sermons 114, 173
urgency in preaching 118

variation in tone 240
verbs 237, 238; use of 191-193
victory 167
vocabulary 235; speaking 189; theological 83; writing 189
vocal folds 219, 224, 230
vocation 28
voice 44, 46; of the church 136; pitch 220; production of 219-220, 223-224; quality of 226-228; use of 219-237

vowel sounds 229
vowels 229-230
Wallace, Bill 120
Weatherspoon, Jesse Burton 201
Williams, Roger 120
Williams, William Carlos 138
witness 31, 247
woman at the well 81-82
word assimilation 235
word(s), human 17, 20, 33, 37; choice of 184, 191, 210; power of 33
study 113
Word 6, 21, 33, 35, 37, 43, 45, 46, 47, 48, 94, 105, 130, 144; authenticity of 218; as deed 2; as event 3; of God 2, 4, 6, 15, 19, 20, 149; of grace 43, 61; as message 2; living 49, 145; made flesh 210; ministry of 7; power of 25, 37; preached 48; proclaimed 51, 61; revealed 6; of Scripture 43; Service of 149; as speech 3; spoken 16, 47, 70, 213, 214; weight of 214, 215, 216
work, pastoral 37
world 27, 154; contemporary 20, 109, 131-137
worry 160
worship 14, 15, 19, 27, 60, 135; acts of 19; corporate 19, 42, 43, 63-64; definition 42; form of 12; individual 42; leader of 242-243; Old Testament 81; service of 19
worshiper 19, 47
wrath of God 5, 8
writing 144, 208-210; discipline of 192
Wycliffe, John 13-14, 120

Zacchaeus 197-198
Zedekiah 5
Zwingli, Huldreich 14

# Scripture Index

Genesis 1—3  165
  1:1  116
  1:3  2
  2:9  182
  2:19  182
  12:1  67
  12—50  158
  22:1-19  123
  28—50  158

Exodus 30:11-14  6

Deuteronomy 6:4  93

Judges 9:7-15  116

1 Samuel 3:9  52

2 Samuel 13:1 to 19:8  161
  18:24 to 19:8  161

Nehemiah 8  7

Psalm 1:2  130
  1:3-4  200
  8:1  130
  8:3  130
  19:1-2  202
  23  153
  27:1  172
  102  225

  119:105  202
  139:6  59
  150  225

Isaiah 1:18  202
  7  6
  9  6
  11  6
  40:3  8
  52:13 to 53:12  29
  53:2  202
  61:1-2  189

Jeremiah 1:7  3
  1:9  35
  20:9  3, 35
  23  34
  23:29  2
  37:17  5

Ezekiel 6:1  2

Daniel 7  123

Matthew 4:1-14  162
  4:17  8
  5:1-13  157
  5:13-14  200
  5:14-16  121
  5:17  157
  5:21 *ff.*  157

6:25-34   161
7:29   100
11:7-15   8
13   160
13:9   52, 75
13:24b   84
14:1-12   8
16:18   160
22:37   32
24:37 ff.   119
25:1-13   124, 160
26:36-46   107
28:19-20a   vii
28:19-20   205

Mark 1:2-8   7-8
1:22   100
1:38   3, 8
4:26-29   108
10:45   29
12:37   74

Luke 2:52   26
4:1-14   162
4:16   26
4:16-30   189
4:16-21   3, 7, 8, 149
4:18-19   9
9:2   18
10:1-20   18, 166
10:1 ff.   18
10:16   52
10:25-27   124
13:34   203
15:11   172
18:9-14   112
24:46-48   vii
24:47   9

John 1   93
1:6-7   7
1:14   2
1:19-42   8
1:29   7

3   71
3:1-15   152
3:1 ff.   169
3:3   152
3:16   160
3:30   8
4:26   82
6:60 ff.   169
7:46   74
10   238
10:11-18   153
12:21   52
14:6   169, 180
14:16   32
14:17   144
16:7-16   160
16:13-14   32
16:13   144
17   137
20:21   8

Acts 1:8   vii
2:14-40   9
2:14   vii
2:38   vii, 136-137
2:40   vii
3:19   9
4:12   137
4:31   viii
5:20   viii
5:29   136
5:41   viii
6   149
6:7   17
9:1-19   9
9:19-20   10
10:1-43   9
13:1   30
13:4-5   10
13–20   11
16:31   169
17:18   37
20:28   26

## Scripture Index

Romans 1:16   38
  1:20-23   68-69
  2:6-11   66
  3:23   159
  4   152
  4:1-25   119
  5:8   160
  5:12-21   124
  6:20-23   67
  6:23   159
  7   141
  8:13   203
  8:21   68
  8:38-39   189
  9:3   69
  9:38-39   189
  10:9   93
  10:14   51
  10:17   51
  11:33   68
  12:2   206
  14:17-18   66

1 Corinthians 2:2   32
  3:16   162
  6:16   162
  9:19   203
  15:22   200
  15:55   200
  15:55-56   239

2 Corinthians 2:16   4
  4:8 *ff.*   121
  4:14   18
  4:18-19   16
  4:18   202
  5:14   35
  5:16-21   193
  8:9   200
  11:23-28   203

Galatians 6:17   206

Ephesians 2:1-10   169-170
  2:8-9   113
  4   52
  4:4-6   200
  4:25   52
  4:29   52
  5:22 to 6:4   165

Philippians 3:13   31
  4:8   202
  4:11   121

Colossians 1:15-20   223
  2:6-7   31
  3   165
  4:2-6   227

1 Thessalonians 1   136
  2:4   3
  2:13   2

2 Timothy 3:16   94
  4:2-5   10
  4:6-8   156

Hebrews 1:1-2   3

James 1:22   51
  2:17-26   113

1 Peter 1:1-2   11
  3:10-17   165
  4:1-4   26, 31
  5:1-4   11

1 John 1:2   192

Revelation 4:1-11   124